S0-BYQ-109

The Wilderness Home of the Giant Panda

The Wilderness Home of the Giant Panda

William G. Sheldon

Illustrations by Russ W. Buzzell

UNIVERSITY OF MASSACHUSETTS PRESS   AMHERST   1975

Library of Congress Catalog Card Number 74-21245

ISBN 0-87023-179-0

Printed in the United States of America

Color frontispiece courtesy

of the Frederic C. Walcott Memorial Fund of

the North American Wildlife Foundation

Library of Congress Cataloging in Publication Data

Sheldon, William G

   The wilderness home of the giant panda.

   Bibliography: p.

   Includes index.

   1. Giant panda.   I.   Title.

QL737.C27S48   599'.74443   74–21245

ISBN 0–87023–179–0

To the memory of Dean Sage, Jr. and T. Donald Carter

Acknowledgements

I am indebted to the World Wildlife Fund for a grant defraying some of the expense in preparing this volume. This organization was approached by C. R. Gutermuth, who encouraged me to write about the habitat of the Giant Panda, basing my account on an expedition to western China.

Several people read various drafts of the manuscript making constructive suggestions. Among them were Robert McLung, Laura Doeringer, James Trefethen, and two anonymous reviewers for the University of Massachusetts Press. Ms. Angela Turnbull completed a very competent and thorough task of editing the final manuscript.

I wish to thank Larry Collins, the chief custodian of the two live Giant Pandas at the National Zoo in Washington. He and his keepers were highly cooperative, enabling me to observe the pandas without crowds and providing me with much valuable information.

Mrs. Anne Sage Holmes supplied me with a copy of the journals of her late husband, Dean Sage, Jr., who was a member of our expedition.

Mr. James Greenway of the American Museum of Natural History spent much of his valuable time assisting me in the identification of the various birds seen or collected on the expedition. People on the Museum mammal staff helped in the identification of the mammals. Some of the latter—particularly voles, have yet to be properly classified to species.

Mr. George Schaller provided me much new information from his current study on blue sheep.

I am indebted to Russell Buzzell for the artwork and to A. Gioiosa for the map.

Mrs. Lee Campbell very ably did the bulk of the typing of the four or five drafts of the manuscript.

I am deeply grateful to my wife, Louise, without whose help and encouragement this volume would never have been finished.

Contents

x
Contents

Illustrations

Preface

In 1934–35 few conservationists were concerned about "endangered species." Nothing was truly known about the giant panda—its classification in the animal kingdom, its habits and habitat in the wild, or its populations. None had been captured alive. While hunting or searching for pandas we made a conscientious effort to learn what we could of this great beast and, for the sake of science, to collect at least one complete specimen for the anatomists to study. Several papers were published as a result of studies made of a female giant panda we brought back. There was no assurance at the time that native hunters would procure a giant panda or many of the other specimens we collected.

As would be necessary in any relatively unknown part of the world, one of our primary tasks was to determine, by collecting specimens, what species of vertebrates existed there. The challenge of looking for the giant panda and other rare species required weeks of searching under almost impossible weather conditions.

We have learned today that the giant panda has a restricted range in western China, compared to the habitat of large vertebrates sharing the panda's range but spreading far beyond.

The purpose of this volume is to place on record a description of the ecology and status of the giant panda as it was forty years ago. This should provide a yardstick to measure changes, at least in habitat, in the last few decades.

Possible dangers to the giant panda are discussed, and a study program proposed to learn accurately its status today.

Because the giant panda is a unique mammal and of great appeal to the public, it has become a status symbol for zoos; it has also become a political animal, being donated by China to several foreign countries. Its popularity could be its undoing. The American and other world conservationists should commend and encourage China in their current efforts to protect the giant panda, provide effective law enforcement in a giant panda sanctuary that has been created, and continue research in their initially successful methods of breeding giant pandas in captivity.

Introduction

The plain of western Szechwan Province in western China, with its teeming human population, is divided from the plateau of Tibet by a formidable mountain mass—the home of the giant panda. Although these ranges are a southeastern extension of the main titans of the Himalayas, they are geologically more ancient, with an origin six hundred thousand years ago in the last stage of the Pleistocene era.

These mountains are composed of some shale, limestone, sandstone, and outcrops of granite.

The hot westerly winds from the Szechwan plain pile up against the mountains of the Chinese-Tibetan borderland where the moisture is condensed, creating a climate of constant rain, fog, and heavy snow. I could find no figures on the annual precipitation above eight thousand feet, but it must exceed one hundred inches a year.

Temperatures vary according to altitude, latitude, and longitude. We experienced a temperature of 0°F. at about fourteen thousand feet in December at timber line. No doubt the tops of the mountains further northwest would have extreme temperatures. In the main giant panda country temperatures were relatively mild, seldom getting below 15° above zero F. in the middle of winter.

Beginning in late November and probably extending to mid-February, when most of the precipitation is snow, the atmosphere is relatively clear compared to the fog, mist, and rain in the warmer months of the year.

The area we investigated is at longitude 103°17.5″ East and latitude 31° 22.5″ North.

The topography, with the exception of river bars, is all very steep, with slopes from thirty degrees to sixty degrees. There were no lakes or ponds even in the mountain basins in the Wassu area we visited.

This vast wilderness of mountain peaks thrusting eighteen to twenty thousand feet above sea level, with deep-cleft cavernous valleys and torrential streams, harbors an extraordinary array of wild fauna, some confined to the high grasslands and rocky peaks above timber line, some to a band of rhododendron trees at timber line, others to the extensive forests of alpine bamboo studded with evergreens arising from the valley floors. Although bamboo is the dominant plant in the lower reaches, there is a variety and juxtaposition of plants characteristic of any area in the world productive of a variety of birds and mammals. Scattered hardwood trees, openings in the forests, and heavy underbrush are attributes of a habitat attractive to many wild species.

The late Dr. Glover M. Allen, the eminent mammalogist, states in his monumental *Mammals of China and Mongolia:* "By far the most interesting and remarkable of the faunal divisions of China is that of the western highlands from approximately southern Kansu and southern Shensi southward to include Szechuan and parts of northern Yunnan and probably Kweichow." He points out that during the Pleistocene era there was no way boreal mammals, if pushed south by the advancing glaciers in the north, could cross the east-west deserts of the Gobi and central Asia. As a result the western highlands became the home of peculiar types that died out elsewhere.

So steep is this magnificent land that when I stepped out of my tent door at an altitude of six thousand feet I could look almost vertically and perceive in one glance four thousand feet of bamboo forest blending into rhododendrons at timber line near twelve thousand feet, grass-covered cliffs to fifteen thousand feet, topped by rocky peaks piercing the sky at eighteen thousand feet or more.

Forbidding as much of the terrain is, there are a mystery and a beauty about this ancient land that cast a spell over any visitor sensitive to wild lands. To the wilderness lover, the curious scientist or hunter, this principality of Wassu challenges the hardihood of the venturesome and the powers of observation of the naturalist.

Many of the spectacular mammals, excepting the blue sheep above timber line and goral of lower altitudes, forage for food at night. Abundant and varied as the wildlife is, it is singularly inconspicuous because of its jungle habitat and its nocturnal or twilight activities.

In such a land the hardy giant panda has lived almost unknown to the Western world for thousands of years.

This book is a description of my experiences of several months climbing in rain, mist, snow, and fog—ever climbing as I studied and sought this ancient mammal. Although forty years have elapsed since this trip, I wrote a full journal every day, often by candlelight and sometimes by firelight. No account would be adequate without a description of other mammals and a great variety of birds sharing the haunts of the giant panda.

Here is a land more virgin than Africa to the hunter and biologist. Besides the famous panda nothing is really known about the fabulous golden monkey or the goat-antelope family, including the Szechwan golden takin, *yea gnu* (wild cow), serow and goral. Packs of wild dogs hunt assiduously at night, predators never studied in the wild. The same can be said for the leopard, several varieties of smaller cats, wild boars, and such rarities as the musk deer, tufted deer or fruit-eating marten. A host of smaller animals caught by our traps are unstudied. Many birds, such as the regal mountain Chinese Monal pheasant, other pheasants, and a variety of additional avian species, have not been investigated in the field.

When we were on this trip in 1934–35 no trained Chinese zoologists had ever made studies in the region. My latest information is that there are Chinese zoologists active in the area today, but I have been unable to find out the extent of their studies.

The books by Desmond Morris (*Men and Pandas*, 1966), Richard Perry (*The World of the Giant Panda*, 1969), and Larry R. Collins and James K. Page, Jr. (1972) contain detailed documentation of what is known of the history of the panda. To avoid redundancy I present below a brief summary of their findings.

Apparently skins of the giant panda from Liangchow, Szechwan, were paid in tribute to Yu over four thousand years ago. According to Morris the early history is vague, but there is little question that the giant panda occurred in Chinese chronicles by 650 A.D., during the reign of the first Chinese emperors.

That remarkable missionary explorer, Père David, who penetrated the far interior of China between 1862 and 1874, opened the door to knowledge of the fauna and flora of western China. Many animals he discovered still bear his name. A noted example was Père David's deer; he transported live ones to Europe, where they were preserved from extinction and have since been reintroduced to Asia.

In 1869 he saw the first skins of a giant panda, which he took to be a new kind of bear. He sent a description of the panda to Alphonse Milne-Edwards in Paris, who was to become director of the Paris Natural History Museum. Milne-Edwards called the panda *Ursus melanoleucus.* Today it has been reclassified as *Ailuropoda melanoleuca.*

The skins, shipped to Paris by David, were the first seen or described by scientists in the western world.

M. M. Berezouski saw giant panda skins on the border of Szechwan and Kansu between 1884 and 1887. He also reported one killed by natives in the Yangliupa district.

Other early explorers in the twentieth century such as Lieutenant J. W. Brooke, Brigadier General J. E. Pereira, and J. H. Edgar sent back reports of the panda. Unfortunately Brooke was killed by a tribe of Lolos while searching for pandas in 1910. Both Pereira and Edgar reported seeing a white animal curled up in the fork of a tree. These *may* have been giant pandas. Edgar's observation was west of the known range of the giant panda.

During World War I a young German zoologist, Hugo Weigold, a member of the Stoetzner expedition of 1914 to west China and east Tibet, spent many days in panda habitat in Wassu pursuing the panda with native dogs, as our expedition did in 1934. Although unsuccessful, the native hunters brought him a live young *bei shung* ("white bear"—giant panda), which shortly died from lack of proper food. Weigold accompanied Brooke Dolan on his trip to giant panda country in 1931.

In April 1928 Theodore Roosevelt, Jr., and his brother, Kermit, shot a large male panda in Yehli, over one hundred miles south of the Wassu country. This was the first panda shot by a white man. In 1931 another German zoologist, Ernst Schäfer, a member of the Dolan Expedition of the Philadelphia Academy of Sciences, shot a baby panda out of a tree in Wassu land; it was in the same valley and the same area we shot one in 1934 and the English Captain H. C. Brocklehurst another in 1935. Quentin Young, a Chinese American, later shot two more.

Although skins reached Western museums, scientists were particularly anxious to examine a complete carcass to clarify the classification of this strange mammal.

Dean Sage and I shot the third panda in Wassu on December 8, 1934, preserving the entire viscera as well as the skin, skull, and parts of the skeleton. Zoologists from the American Museum of Natural History published scientific papers on this material, further adding fuel to the eventual controversy over the classification of the panda. In 1936 Mrs. Ruth Harkness secured a very young giant panda in Wassu country and successfully fed it and brought it to America, the first live panda seen in the Western world. Following her success, the giant panda became a status symbol for zoos all over the world. As well as I can determine seventeen giant pandas were shipped to Western countries before 1972. All of these have died. A male and female were donated by China to the United States and shipped to Washington, D.C. in 1972 and appear to be thriving.

Although accurate figures are not obtainable, about twenty live giant pandas have been captured and distributed to zoos in different Chinese cities. China recently donated two giant pandas to Japan, two to Korea and two to England. The best news of all is that the Chinese have successfully bred captured pandas in the Peking Zoo. Ten cubs have been born but only two survived.

Probably a number of live pandas captured in recent years perished for lack of proper care and food before they ever arrived in Chengtu or other destinations in China. Perry reported that besides the live pandas about sixty skins were sent to the West in relatively recent times. A conservative estimate of pandas known to have been killed or captured alive between 1925 and 1972 would be one hundred or more. An unknown number have been killed in native spear traps. Until 1935 at least, farmer-hunters could pay the prince of Wassu one takin skin or one giant panda skin for annual taxes.

Reviewers of this text have raised important questions such as why I have delayed for forty years in writing this book, and what changes may have occurred since 1934–35.

I published a short scientific summary in 1938. Since then I received scientific training and thus could interpret some of my field observations more accurately. Also, books on the giant panda deal almost exclusively with zoo captives. The giant panda is considered an endangered species, and I felt it was highly important to describe the wild habitat and speculate on the dangers both to the habitat and this animal itself.

To the best of my knowledge, no Westerner has penetrated these wild mountains since before World War II. Some Westerners may have travelled the main caravan routes on the perimeter of panda country, but I have not found any published reports. There are no other roads across most of the panda range.

Even in the event that serious alterations have occurred in this country, my descriptions of habitat and populations would provide a yardstick against which to measure changes over forty years. Apparently the Chinese consider it still to be good panda habitat since they have established a wildlife preserve in the Min range northeast of the country we visited.

To the best of my knowledge it is the only description in some detail of the giant panda habitat.

The Wilderness Home of the Giant Panda

Panda habitat

Chapter One

Expedition Organization

LISTEN! Do you hear the dogs?" I asked; Sage replied "This is hopeless. The dogs are going far down the valley." Clinging to ice-covered ledges three thousand feet above our camp on one of the last days of our expedition, we had released several dogs in the dense bamboos in Chengwei Valley, deep in the wild mountains of western China. Suddenly the dogs sounded closer. With suppressed excitement we strained our eyes to penetrate the dense bamboos. Crashing through the bamboos a pursued animal gave a deep growl. One of my Chinese hunters said "Paotzu" (leopard). In another few seconds he saw his mistake and corrected the name, calling it *"Bei shung"*; a ghostlike black and white animal, the giant panda we had been seeking for so many months, appeared fifty yards below me leisurely walking, surrounded by barking dogs, and headed directly for Dean Sage on a cliff lower down.

This was the culmination of the Sage West China Expedition to Szechwan Province in western China for the American Museum of Natural History in 1934–35.

The objectives of the expedition were not only to collect a large series of representative mammals and birds from this section of China but to study the habitat and behavior of the giant panda.

The plan was hatched as Dean Sage, a law student at Harvard, was sitting before a warm fire in the first frosts of autumn in 1933, and listening enthralled to his friend Brooke Dolan's account of his experiences in giant panda country in 1931. Dolan, through the auspices of the Philadelphia Academy of Sciences, had visited this country in 1931 accompanied by Hugo Weigold and Ernst Schäfer, two German zoologists. Weigold was the first Westerner to penetrate these particular mountains, as early as 1913, but as far as we knew, no other Westerners had spent any time deep in these ranges.

Sage and his wife Anne were veterans of big game hunting in Africa and Alaska and well equipped to undertake such a trip to the other side of the world. Dean Sage was an avid outdoorsman. The law later proved not to be his cup of tea and he ran a cattle ranch in Wyoming for many years before his death in 1964. Sage was full of enthusiasm, highly articulate, and an attractive personality, a fine companion for what proved to be a difficult and sometimes hazard-

Sage with the skull of a bull takin   *Anne Sage*

Carter

The author

Mr. Fung   *Jim*

ous expedition. As leader of the expedition he handled most of the problems of finance and diplomacy necessary to get permission from Chinese authorities to enter this territory.

His wife, Anne, deserves much of the credit for the success of this trip in amassing 2,700 mammals and 500 bird specimens for the museum collection. She had been trained in preparing scientific specimens for the museum and in turn trained many of our porters, supervising these assistants with great efficiency. Due to the misfortune of badly damaging her knee on the first day of our foot trek she cheerfully remained in camp much of the time to promote our collection, but in spite of her knee made some remarkable climbs in the high country. I never heard her complain and she was always the most optimistic of all of us.

Since the Sages wanted to make this trip, in contrast to their other expeditions, one that would contribute to scientific knowledge, they affiliated themselves with the American Museum of Natural History in New York. The museum sent with us the veteran naturalist, mammalogist, and field collector, T. Donald Carter, a man of even disposition, humor, and with a warm personality. He was an indefatigable worker. Carter had the best general knowledge of birds and mammals in the world of any scientist I have known. He had collected in many parts of Africa, South America, and elsewhere in his busy career. He suffered what was apparently a mild heart attack at our high altitude camp but willingly descended to a lower camp and ran his own collecting outpost for several weeks, joining us later in the giant panda valley. He was fully dedicated to the objectives of the expedition.

I can well remember after working all week in a logging camp in the rugged canyon country under the shadow of Mount St. Helens in western Washington picking up my mail at the main camp on a weekend to find a letter from Dean Sage inviting me to go to western China as assistant collector for the expedition. I was startled and wasted little time wiring an acceptance. My qualifications were my experience in studying the distribution of northern mountain sheep in British Columbia for three summers. I had collected and had prepared small mammals and birds for museums from boyhood. Little did I realize that my fall and winter of rugged work in the rainy wet forests of the West resulted in the best physical condition of my life in preparation for climbing and traveling in the even wetter jungles on the other side of the world.

All of us were in our early twenties except Carter, who was forty-four.

Other key people, Chinese, joined our group later in China. We were accompanied by a Mr. Fung to act as interpreter. He was a pleasant young man, speaking poor English and totally out of his realm in the mountains. Our most valuable man was our cook, "Jim," who spoke good English. He had worked on an American gunboat and had been to Europe. Since he had learned English working on the gunboat he had a rich infusion of profanity in his speech which he assumed was proper language. His ability at handling the coolies forcefully and providing for our quarters and meals was truly remarkable.

Other important people were the Chinese hunters, who will be described later in this volume.

I returned to the East in March 1934 and became deeply engaged drawing up inventories and collecting equipment for the expedition. Dean sent me to Washington to talk with Far Eastern people in the state department, describing the purposes of our trip and obtaining letters to the ambassador and consulate people in China.

Carter and I preceeded the Sages by two months. Boarding the freighter *City of Elwood* in New York on April 23, 1934, we sailed with all our equipment to Shanghai via the Panama Canal, Hawaii, and the Philippine Islands. We reached Shanghai on June 30.

The political climate in China at that period required endless red tape. Our first task was to apply for passports from the Nanking government to enter the interior. We shortly learned that things cannot be hurried in China. I visited Nanking on several occasions to drink tea with the minister responsible for our passports. The Sages arrived on July 25. All necessary papers and arms permits were finally granted on August 15.

After months of planning and dreaming we had overcome our first hurdle, but the delay was frustrating; however, one has to learn quickly to accept such setbacks in China with understanding.

Houses of stone in a Ch'iang village

Chapter Two

Approaching the gateway to the land of the giant panda

OUR first destination was Chunking, 1,500 miles up the Yangtze River. We boarded the small American steamship, S.S. *Chiping*, on August 17 and soon discovered the "Yangtze Rapid Steamship Company" was a misnomer. Our boat was probably the slowest in the fleet.

We lived in small staterooms on the upper deck with an armed guard of five Marines. Noisy Chinese were jammed in the lower deck. We anchored at a town every night and the stench of opium from the lower deck became almost nauseating.

There was an American captain, but all navigation of the river, becoming treacherous in its upper reaches, was done by a skilled Chinese river pilot.

The first thousand miles traversed from Shanghai to Ichang, at the mouth of the great gorge of the Yangtze, as viewed from the deck of a river steamer, was largely agricultural and somewhat monotonous. The river was flanked by vast plains broken here and there by lone bluffs or ridges. Small mountainous hills were often visible in the distance. Precipitous rocky walls near the shore, conspicuous because of their isolation, were often surmounted by ancient pagodas.

Hamlets or large villages surrounded by small farms were almost continually in sight. The methods of farming in China at that time were very different from farming in the Western world. There was no mechanization. The Chinese peasant tilled his soil and irrigated his rice fields with human manure as his forefathers had done for countless generations. His house was usually made from a composition of mud and bamboo, dirty in the extreme as measured by Western standards.

Many Chinese junks, the paramount water craft used by the natives, were continuously in sight.

In five days we reached Ichang, where we had to wait for two days until the water dropped to a low enough level to admit the passage up the famous Yangtze Gorge.

This was my first opportunity to observe a city largely uninfluenced by any foreigners. Although Japanese, American, and English gunboats were anchored in front of the town and the Standard Oil Company had a large plant, there were few foreign buildings. What impressed me the most was the intense concentration of the population. When seen at a distance the town did not appear very large but once I penetrated the city streets I was quickly disillusioned. The poverty and filth were most depressing. Whole families seemed to live in single rooms separated from each other by thin partitions of bamboo matting. Their homes were shared by dogs and chickens. Most of the babies ran around naked and many showed signs of bad skin diseases. The number of inhabitants suffering from crippled limbs, malformed bodies, and chronic ailments was astonishing. Sewers were unknown, all the refuse being carried to the edges of town to fertilize the fields or feed hogs.

There seemed to be an endless, restless coming and going of the coolies. The chant of the Chinese coolie as he perspires and labors under a heavy burden is one of the most familiar sounds—a cry that has always been a part of China. Junks of all varieties congregated around our ship and there was a ceaseless jabber of talk, most of the participants straining at the tops of their lungs to make themselves heard.

As it was the middle of Chinese July many lanterns constructed of wood, paper, and candles floated past us at night. A Chinese priest with his idols constructed of bamboo covered by paper held a noisy ceremony beside our boat so she might be protected by the river gods during our trip up river. There were firecrackers, the clanging of cymbals, and a constant chant of the priest.

During the last evening in Ichang our very drunk captain called Dean and Carter into his cabin. He said that Floyd Smith, the animal collector from the Chicago Field Museum, was held captive by bandits on the edge of Tibet in Tatsienlu and would never come out alive. This was a false report. He said that if we went beyond Chengtu we would be cut off by armies of the war-lord of Szechwan, Liu Hsiang.

During the afternoon before the captain became inebriated he had unloaded a good deal of cargo to enable the boat to surmount the rapids in the gorge; after he fell asleep a number of sampans came along side and loaded the boat with contraband freight.

At 3:00 A.M. the anchors began to drag. The stern of our boat was sixty feet from shore. As it started to swing in, it could have demolished all the junks and sampans along the bank. The Marines could not wake the captain up. The disaster was averted by the combined efforts of the Chinese pilot and boatswain. On Sunday morning, August 26, I was awakened by the start of the engines. We were once more on our way.

Horse transport, Min River Valley

Chinese junk in Yangtze River Gorge

Ichang lies at the mouth of the spectacular Yangtze Gorge, and we immediately went out on deck to enjoy our first view of scenic China. I was not disappointed in my anticipation of the grandeur of one of the most famous natural sights of China. From each bank of the river precipitous cliffs reared up abruptly to heights varying from one thousand to three thousand feet—so steep in places that they appeared to fairly overhang the mighty river below. The varied shades of red and yellow sandstone and limestone were beautiful. Vegetation was generally sparse, although on some slopes it was very thick but stunted. One could not help but gain the impression of aridity and barrenness.

The great power of the chocolate-colored river was immediately apparent. Pinched between rocky banks scarcely more than four hundred feet apart, it reaches depths of over one hundred feet. It presented a spectacle of a vast cauldron of tremendous whirlpools, confusing eddies, and heavy rapids.

Along the rock walls of each side was a trail hewn out and worn smooth by countless generations of Chinese; it was their only means of tracking their junks upstream. I was struck by the antiquity of the villages nestled in the hills with their own temples. It was fascinating to realize the number of years the Chinese have been tracking their junks up the Yangtze and building their temples and worshipping their idols.

The ruthlessness of the stream was made manifest by the not infrequent sight of a corpse wafted along by the current.

Large junks of extremely excited Chinese with twenty men manning the oars swept by us down the rapids. We saw junks of similar size moving upstream pulled by a large number of naked river coolies, known as Szechwan *bares*, tugging and straining at the end of a long rope.

The scene was tremendous, impressive and beautiful.

Engine trouble forced us to stop, swing about, and proceed downstream to the village of Hsiang Chih, where we anchored for the night.

Dean and I climbed a hill above the town in the afternoon. What astonished me in that country was how completely the natives have improvised every square foot of land for cultivation. Corn-fields are planted on slopes of forty-five degrees. The highest corn-fields were under overhanging cliffs near the summits of the mountains. Corn, today a staple crop in the wilder country of west China, must have been introduced in the sixteenth century by traders.

We walked through an old temple, where an ancient Chinese man offered us a pipe of tobacco, opium, a cigarette, or tea. Due to the unsanitary aspects of these offerings we ran the risk of offending the old gentleman by our refusal.

I saw two of the native women with bound feet, so tiny they could scarcely walk. I saw many old women throughout my stay in China who were tortured by this barbaric custom. However, I understood it was out of vogue and forbidden by the National regime. I did not see a young girl thus crippled for life.

The junks surrounding the ship each night were manned by coolies of filthy and unsanitary habits. Their voices and conversations sounded almost uncivilized to my ears. To offset such impressions they seemed happy and cheerful no matter how difficult might be their task. I heard the estimate that eighty percent of the natives in this part of China, at that time, were opium addicts. The fumes of the opium pipes smoked by the Chinese passengers on the deck below us or the junks alongside the boat were sickening.

In pouring rain we proceeded to Kweifu for the night. One of the Yangtze Rapid Steamship Company's boats had been wrecked not far from there a few weeks before our arrival and the captain was living there on a Chinese junk until she was salvaged. He reported the daily execution of Communists in the town and told of rumors of the National troops coming up to make war on Liu Hsiang, the war-lord of Szechwan.

We saw no wild mammals except bats. The commonest birds were brown kites. We also saw blue herons, egrets, and orioles.

One of the most interesting of the Yangtze Gorges is the "box gorge". Coffins were deposited in small crevices over a hundred feet up the sides of apparently unscalable perpendicular cliffs. They had been there for the past fifteen years, and no one seemed to know how the Chinese did it.

At Kweifu we had passed out of the gorges. The river was bordered by steep ravines and hills cut by clear mountain streams flowing into the Yangtze. The river was broader and the shore was covered with arable soil even on steep slopes.

At our next stop, we were at the gateway of Szechwan Province.

The military situation in Szechwan during the time of our visit was critical. Chiang Kai-shek, the ruler of China, had sent troops to attack Liu Hsiang, the war-lord of Szechwan, to depose him and deprive him of his autonomous rule of this province, for many years not under the control of the central government in Nanking. We kept hearing reports of clashes between these two armies. Apparently it was all settled by an enormous bribe paid to Liu Hsiang by Nanking rulers. At the same time Communist troops were moving west in northern Shensi Province, and the central government also was sending armies there to stop their invasion. While rumors of all kinds were prevalent, there was some danger the Communist troops would eventually reach the city of Chengtu during our trip into the mountains, so we were kept apprised by runners of the military situation during our whole trip.

We arrived in the city of Chungking on the morning of August 31. Situated on the top of a high hill, steep tiers of stone steps have been trod by Chinese for thousands of years to the city above.

When I was on the dock clearing our equipment I counted thirty corpses of adults and some children drifting grotesquely by in the river current. Life seemed cheap in China and there was little concern with what might have been the fate of these unfortunate people. The streets were filthy, full of beggars, cripples, and polluted by opium dens. We were held up there for several days clearing all our equipment through customs and getting a further travel permit from the war lord of the province to proceed to the interior.

On September 6 we left Chungking in a new Ford driven by Mr. Schukard, a trader who was en route to Chengtu. The two days of travel to Chengtu was a hazardous trip. The driver had had little experience, and it was very fortunate that we did not hit the many coolies and other people on the road since Mr. Schukard usually just blew the horn and stepped on the gas when crowds appeared ahead of him.

We arrived at Chengtu on September 8. We were comfortably put up in the house of missionaries, the Reverend and Mrs. F. Dickinson of West China Union University. These wonderful people not only kept us informed throughout our mountain sojourn of the military situation in China but also arranged for the coolies to depart from Chengtu en route to the gateway of the mountains.

We stayed at their house until September 11 packing our equipment. We had to make loads of about forty-five pounds each. It was necessary to weigh each one as these coolies' method of carrying was the common one of balancing two loads on the ends of a bamboo cross pole. The coolies departed at daybreak on the morning of September 10 with the first stop at Kwanshien. We planned to follow the next day by car. There was nothing but foot travel beyond this town.

Goral

Chapter Three

Entering the realm of
the giant panda

MUCH has been written about the inaccessibility of the giant panda range. Actually in 1934 it was possible to fly by plane from Shanghai to Chengtu, travel one day by car to Kwanshien, and, depending on the rate of foot travel, reach the best giant panda country in two or three days. The distance from Kwanshien to the heart of the giant panda valley was sixty-five miles.

Two other members joined our party in Chengtu. One was Mr. Fung, who was described in the first chapter and supposed to be our interpreter, and the other was "Jim," our cook.

All six of us with our weapons and a little personal luggage were packed in a Ford Cabriolet to drive thirty-six miles to Kwanshien. We started just before noon headed west across the Chengtu plains. The latter are very flat and renowned for their rich fertility, watered by irrigation canals from the Min River. This is probably the most famous and oldest engineering feat in China. At Kwanshien the main stream is split into many channels by dikes guiding the water evenly over the entire plain. A drought has not been recorded in two thousand years. The Min River flows from the mountains and maintains an even flow.

When we arrived in Kwanshien we found that our coolies had gone ahead of us. We spent the night at the mission and set off the next day as early as possible. We had to hire four other coolies to take the equipment we had brought in the car and Dean also hired two chairs since it was our first day on foot. He and Anne went ahead with Jim (the cook), and one chair. Carter, Fung, and I remained behind with the other chair and four coolies who had our equipment. The trail led up the Min River.

"Trail" is hardly adequate to describe the pathway we pursued. The route was a stone road with large stone slabs serving for steps wherever there was a slight hill. A few miles up the river we passed ornate arches, the usual Chinese architecture, on each side of a temple courtyard. Such old structures with numerous small Buddha statues, stone images, and stone slabs with Chinese inscriptions were seen frequently during the day. Whenever the river flowed through a gorge the trail ascended, passing over a steep bordering hill, then dropped down to the river level again. Our coolies seemed very slow; since I had no previous experience with such carriers I was reluctant to urge them on at a more rapid pace.

We came to a village about every three miles. They all resembled each other, with a narrow, stone-paved main street bordered by one-story mud houses with pigs and mangy dogs gathering what they were able to find in the swill-littered road. There were a few chickens, geese, and ducks. Although the inhabitants of these towns must have seen many foreigners they never ceased to show great curiosity. The children often followed behind yelling "yang-zo," literally meaning "large nose."

The further we progressed into the mountains the more striking the natives appeared. I think this is probably due to the influence of a more enervating climate and the intrusion of different genes from the Tibetans and tribes of people to the north and west. The women especially had more attractive features than any I had seen in China.

Although many coolies carried their loads by the bamboo cross pole, those coming from the north laden with goat skins, medicines, roots and herbs, wooden bowls, and other products used the mountain back pack with shoulder straps and a wooden frame constructed to fit the back. I was quite surprised not to observe any use of a tump line (head strap), for in most parts of the world men have found they can carry heavy loads by thus employing their neck muscles.

Small horses and jackasses coming from the north clambered by us. There was no cinch under the animals' bellies as is customary in packing horses in North America. A saddle with perfectly balanced loads was set on the back of the horse; it had long horns which come well down on the side and a brichen around the chest. These pack animals climbed up and down the steep narrow mountain trails with apparent ease.

Along the lower reaches of the Min, not far above Kwanshien, I saw some Chinese shoveling sand in a sluice, hoping, I presume, to wash a little gold dust. The river was very swift, and Kwanshien probably the height of navigation for any kind of water craft.

We saw corn-fields on the very tops of some of the ridges and steep slopes. The corn was even grown in the fine sand of the river bottoms.

In the late afternoon of the first day of foot travel we turned east from the main river and followed the gorge of a smaller tributary. The trail climbed steeply toward a pass twenty-five hundred feet above the Min River. The unsure footing in the tributary gorge could be extremely dangerous, as one could slip off the outer edge and fall twenty-five hundred feet to the stream bed.

It was truly beautiful. The road was, in places, merely cut out of

A group of the Ch'iang tribesmen living in panda country. Many have an infusion of pure Chinese genes. The clothing is typical.

Expedition en route to panda country. The wooden bowls are one of the exports of the mountain people.

the sides of the cliffs and wound around spurs, up canyons, and across clear mountain brooks. What a relief to see clear water once again, and what a joy to feel the invigorating air of the mountains. The foliage was lovely and refreshing. Everything had the appearance of early autumn—flowers with a few brilliant petals still clinging to their stalks, grass turned tawny brown, corn being harvested on the hillsides, and coolness in the air. The mosses and varieties of ferns were of particular verdancy and added immeasurably to the pleasure of the walk. Along the water's edge we observed river redstarts, a species of wagtail, water ouzels, crows, and rooks.

It proved tiring following our men at such a slow pace. Fung had been using the chair most of the morning, but Don and I preferred to walk to condition ourselves for our mountain traveling. We did not arrive at the summit of the pass until a half-hour before dark, but we were determined to go on as far as possible. Darkness overtook us during our descent. Fortunately I had a flashlight which lighted the way for the coolies and for us; a step over the edge along some of the narrower sections of the trail could have been of extreme danger. We noticed fires here and there high up on the slopes and in the distance, and heard the sound of the natives hitting two sticks together rapidly, probably to keep marauding animals out of the corn-fields.

We descended two thousand feet to a local hovel which could not be called an inn or a house. We were both tired and ready for sleep. The inner man was satisfied by a big sandwich apiece and a bowl of rice. Our bed was a straw mat on bamboo cross slats with a single narrow quilt covering, highly inadequate to keep one warm on a cold night. Don's bed was separated from a pig trough by a thin bamboo partition. The emanating odors of this combined with opium and grunts of the pigs kept us awake much of the night. Furthermore, we were badly bitten by carnivorous insects.

We left at daylight and shortly caught up with the Sages in a village twenty-seven miles north of Kwanshien.

This forced trek, to catch our coolies on the first day, had brought a serious casualty. Anne had badly sprained her knee, which incapacitated her to a greater or lesser degree during the entire trip. However with the knee strapped up she did manage to climb very steep mountains, although in great pain, and certainly showed tremendous courage to keep up with the outfit.

The mountains became more and more precipitous. The river was swifter and the trail poorer. The ranges bordering the valley rose more abruptly and steeply than any I had seen in China with the exception of those along the Yangtze River Gorges, but in spite of some treacherous cliffs the slopes were not unscalable. Vegetation covered them to the very tops, which rose three thousand feet from the river bottom. We passed through a wide, precipitous, verdant canyon.

The valley we passed was clear, but dense fog and mist clung to the crests of the ridges all day. I feared that such diurnal fog would be one of the impediments to successful exploration in the mountains. I had not yet observed thick bamboo growing on the slopes, one of the chief characteristics of the haunts of the giant panda.

Early in the afternoon we arrived at a small village, where we saw a young female Himàlayan black bear tethered near the trail. She was very playful and apparently healthy. There were other indications that we were on the border of wilder country, as we saw the skin of a serow in front of one of the native's shacks, and a crudely stuffed skin of one of the native wildcats. We saw a buzzard for the first time, with light tan shoulders and a dark brown body.

We stopped at the town of Tso Chiao, where we spent the night. This town lies fourteen miles east of the little hamlet of Tsaopo, which was to be used by Mrs. Harkness as her headquarters in 1936. It would be a feasible two-day trek, or a very easy three-day trip, to walk from Kwanshien to Tsaopo.

We went to the town of Wenchwan, ten miles up the main Min, to pay our respects to the wife of the deceased prince of the region, Tso Tousa. We were to discharge our Chengtu coolies and arrange to hire mountain men who carry their burdens on their backs.

As we neared Wenchwan the valley opened up a great deal, and the river bottom became less of a canyon. Poplars, willows, alder, walnut, several fruit trees, and occasionally soap trees were the principal hardwood trees lining the banks or around settlements. Chinese graves were often seen under the trees, for it is one of their beliefs that this burial insures everlasting peace for the deceased. We saw evergreens of several varieties: spruces, silver fir, hemlock-spruce, and pines were present.

Carter and I observed a great titmouse colored very much like our own chickadee. We also observed several magpies, hawks, and wagtails.

In the early afternoon we descended a steep grade where the trail dropped from the cliffs and followed the grassy level shelf along the river to the town of Wenchwan, the center of the principality of Wassu.

I was astonished and pleasantly surprised on entering the gate through the ancient and broken-down city wall to see a narrow, smoothly paved street practically deserted. This was entirely unlooked for in a Chinese town. What people we saw all showed very different physical features from the typical Chinese.

The history of the principality of Wassu and the origins of the people in the area had been documented by J. H. Edgar and T.

Himalayan black bear cub, Min River Valley

Torrance, who were missionaries stationed at West China Missionary University in Cheng Tu.

The mountainous border of China and Tibet is populated by various tribes of people of uncertain origin. The original tribe inhabiting the Wenchwan area and country to the west is called Ch'iang. The principality was established in 1442 A.D.; the first prince was from India and installed by the Ming Dynasty of China to occupy and rule a buffer area between Tibet and China in Szechwan Province. The territory, according to Edgar, including all the area where we conducted our field studies, begins "some miles west of Ta Wih and continues 70 miles to Weichow, encompassing an area with a rough diameter of 80 miles." The most important original center of these people was at Tsaopo, where we saw many fine castles built centuries ago by the Ch'iang.

This principality is bordered on the south by tribes of Lolos, reputed to be far more warlike and unfriendly to Westerners. The more nomadic Hsifan—mostly Tibetan—live north of Wassu. The latter principality had maintained its identity for hundreds of years, and even when we were there battles with bordering peoples had recently taken place. Tso Tousa, the prince, had been killed, and his widow, whom we were to visit, ruled in the area.

She seemed to exert an authority respected by the serflike mountain people. When we arrived runners were sent to all areas in the mountains instructing hunters to spring all dangerous spear traps so the "foreigners" would not be impaled by them.

The people living in the area at the time of our expedition had not maintained their racial identity and there had been an infusion of Chinese and Tibetan characteristics.

Most of the Wassu people lived on farms in the mountains. The main crop was corn but a variety of other vegetables were grown: barley, beans, and potatoes were the most popular. Rice could not be grown in this area and had to be imported from eastern Szechwan. We saw pigs, chickens, and a few cattle in the lower regions, and wild pheasants and large wild mammals were often part of the diet.

Charcoal was made particularly in the winter months. One of the commonest products was a type of wooden bowl fashioned very symmetrically from pieces of spruce. Medicinal roots were collected from the mountains.

I saw few tools. Some mountain people had a crude type of axe resembling a pick more than an axe. I saw one crosscut saw. I brought three axes and the porters and hunters appeared amazed at their effectiveness. The commonest tool in the mountain country was a type of machete with a blade about eight inches long and hooked at the end. The Wassu men carried these on their belts and they were especially good for cutting bamboo.

Princess Tsa Tousa and daughter

The main dwellings were unique stone houses. Perfectly square, forty-five feet on each side, they were erected from large stones cemented together with crude mud plaster. The four walls have a slight inward inclination. About twelve feet above the dirt floor, timbers, each end embedded in the wall, were laid and were surmounted by cross pieces of lighter timber laid close together. The flat roof was composed of a layer of dirt, a foot thick, packed on the cross pieces. There was an entrance door at the bottom of the wall. There were usually three or four rooms. There was an open fire at one end of the largest room and an open stone oven at the other end. One or two very large iron cooking basins were set in the stone.

A ladder ascended from the room to an aperture in the roof, and the opening served also as a chimney. There were no windows on the ground floor. The front of the roof was surrounded with a stone wall about three feet high. The back of the roof-top had an additional board roof and was divided into several sections for storage of beans, corn, grain, and other food products. Several of the houses at different locations served as our camp; we set tents on the dirt of the roof.

Some of these farmers were skilled woodsmen and ardent hunters. Temporary bamboo lean-tos were scattered on the wild bamboo slopes, serving as shelters for hunters or woodcutters.

The only weapons we saw were crude matchlocks, usually loaded with an odd assortment of screws and bolts. We soon learned they were inefficient but once in a while were effective at very close range.

Most hunters had dogs. These were small canines, usually close to the color of a police dog. Except for their color, with their round heads and tails curled over their backs they resembled chows. They could follow a hot trail and chase any animal on four legs, but they lacked persistence and would often give up after a short chase. The longest run I saw was half an hour.

Most of the large mammals obtained were killed by lethal spear traps described in chapter 7. In my judgment, however, the greatest skill of these hunters was their construction of efficient bamboo foot snares. These captured many pheasants and such large mammals as young blue sheep and some of the smaller deer.

In this wild and rugged environment these illiterate people struggled to eke out an existence. Nonetheless, they were friendly, very warm, and often jolly and fun-loving.

Mr. Floyd T. Smith of the Field Museum in Chicago had been working for some months in this region training natives to collect live animals and birds for him. When we met him in Chengtu he very kindly gave us the keys to his temporary dwelling in Wenchwan, the old Catholic mission.

In the inner courtyard two pens contained the following live birds captured for him by the natives: three blood pheasants, one koklass pheasant, one monal pheasant, six tragopan pheasants, and some black-headed hawfinches. What interested me most were six blue sheep or bharal, four ewes and two young rams captured in the region we were to visit above Tsaopo. Three years later Smith brought out five live giant pandas captured by his agents.

Since Mrs. Tso Tousa lived five miles away at Tung-lin Shan, Dean and Anne planned to visit her the next day.

We had become comfortably settled in the roomy quarters of the old mission and prepared to leave as soon as we could collect the mountain coolies.

Dean visited the local magistrate to inform him of our arrival and seek his aid in procuring native hunters and porters.

Anne, Dean, and Fung left early the next morning to cross the river and visit Mrs. Tso Tousa. Don and I walked through the town as far as the bamboo bridge across the river, where I collected a great titmouse, prepared by Don as our first specimen. We saw magpies, crows, wagtails, and some sparrows.

I was much interested to see a number of shrines in the open courtyards along the street. They were filled with Buddhas, figures of other lesser Chinese gods, tablets, and Chinese inscriptions. According to Torrance these people are or were lamas.

In the afternoon, with the help of our cook, I discussed with a few of the natives the habits of the giant panda and the takin. In contrast to many villages visited by Theodore Roosevelt, Jr. and his brother, Kermit, the name *bei shung* was almost a household word in the Wenchwan area, but I reaped little information of any avail to us. One interesting comment made by one of the natives was that young takin were caught by building bamboo nets around a patch of rural woods where these animals occur. Two of these mammals were brought out to Wenchwan the previous spring. All seemed unanimous that the region northwest of Tsaopo was the best wildlife country.

The others returned in the afternoon and reported a successful visit with Mrs. Tso Tousa. She did not go out for meals, it appeared, but welcomed our gifts of Benedictine, scissors, and fountain pen and pencil. Dean also employed her nephew, Kao, as one of our hunters since he knew the country thoroughly. He agreed to leave his gun at home but bring his dogs since the latter could be very useful if trained in trailing game; otherwise we felt they would prove to be a nuisance. The following day we rearranged our equipment to leave a base of supplies in Tsaopo. We sorted out enough food, films, and ammunition to last us the first three weeks, when we would be collecting in the high mountains.

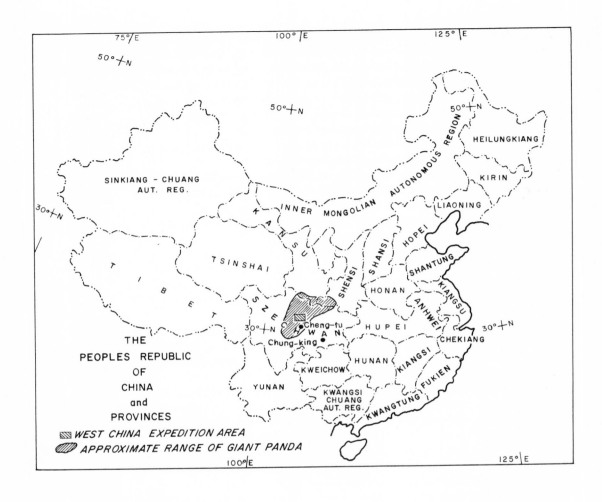

75°/E   100° /E   125° /E

50° +N

50° +N

50° +N

HEILUNGKIANG

SINKIANG - CHUANG AUT. REG.

KIRIN

30° +N

INNER MONGOLIAN AUTONOMOUS REGION

LIAONING

K A N S U

T I B E T

TSINSHAI

HOPEI

SHANTUNG

SHENSI

SHANSI

HONAN

S Z E C H W A N

KIANGSU

ANHWEI

Cheng-tu

HUPEI

30° +N

Chung-king

CHEKIANG

THE

PEOPLES REPUBLIC

OF

CHINA

and

PROVINCES

KWEICHOW

HUNAN

KIANGSI

YUNAN

KWANGSI CHUANG AUT. REG.

FUKIEN

KWANGTUNG

WEST CHINA EXPEDITION AREA

APPROXIMATE RANGE OF GIANT PANDA

100°/E   125° /E

Our proposed itinerary, based on the information given us by Brooke Dolan, was as follows. The first objective was the town of Tsaopo, situated nine miles west of the Min River up the tributary which flows into the main stream at Tso Chiao. A few miles west of Tso Chiao the tributary forks: Tsaopo lies about three miles up the southwest fork while Chengwei is the northwest fork, the best place for takin and giant panda. Further to the northwest are three additional tributaries, one from the Mamogo Valley, another from the Dabeishuigo Valley, and the third from the Yenshuigo Valley where the natives said golden monkeys were found. The mountain range of Chiung Lai Shan is at the headwaters of the branch above Tsaopo. A trail from Tsaopo is the best approach to the range of the blue sheep. There was also a very fair chance of finding takin in the grasslands above the timberline at that time of year (September) provided the weather was clear.

Our work was interrupted about 5:30 P.M. to arrange a dinner for a local magistrate and ten other leading townsmen. A Chinese cook had been hired to prepare Chinese food.

Our first guest arrived a few minutes before 6:00 P.M. attired in a long black Chinese gown and a filthy old woolen cap. the others came in shortly after; the magistrate was the most intelligent and talkative. There was one man, eighty-one years old, a "learned" man according to Fung, who was apparently the old man of the town. One of the nicest looking was the youngest guest, who was a principal of the local school. A few of the others looked rather dissipated and bored. This was the first and only truly Chinese meal I had ever eaten with Chinese men. Mr. Fung acted as our host. When a dish was placed on the table none of the others lifted their chopsticks until he had done so; he also took the initiative in sipping from a bottle of whiskey. It was empty at the end of the evening.

Anne had been spending a great deal of time and labor treating natives who complained of sickness or sores; her fame had spread. One of the first things the magistrate commented on was her medicinal services among his people.

Sage gives an account of a typical dialogue between Anne, Fung, and a patient as follows:

The patient: jabbering and gesticulating.

Fung: "Man say have pain."

Anne: "Where has he pain?"

Fung and patient jabber together. Fung: "He have pain in stomach."

Anne: "How long has he been sick?"

Answer: "Anywhere from one month to three years. Never less than a month."

Anne: "Does eating make him sick?"

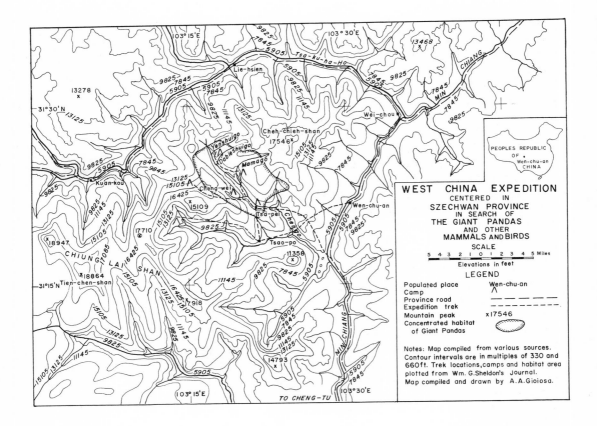

13468

103°15'E   103°30'E

9825
7845
5905   CHIANG
Tsa-ku-ha-Ho
Lie-hsien   5905
9825   9845   9825
9825 7845   MIN
5905 5905   11145   7845
7845   9825   Wei-chou
13278   9825 11145 13125   9825
x   13125
31°30'N 13125   Cheh-chieh-shan
17546 x
Yenshuigo   15105
9825 7845   Dablashuigo   11145
5905   Mamago   9825
9825 9845   7845
13125
Kuan-kou   15105   15105
9825   Cheng-wei
11145 13125   16425   x 9825
15105   15109   15125
18947   17710   5125
x   16425 9825
CHIUNG LAI   17085
18864   15105 SHAN   11358
x   16425   x
31°15'N Tien-chen-shan 15105   11145   7845 5905
13125   16425 13105   9825
13125   x 918   5905
11145   7845
13105   9825
11145
15105 13125   14793   9825 7845
11145   x   5905
15105 13125   MINCHIANG 5905 7845
5905

103°15'E   103°30'E
TO CHENG-TU

<table>
<tr><td colspan="2">**WEST CHINA EXPEDITION**
CENTERED IN
SZECHWAN PROVINCE
IN SEARCH OF
THE GIANT PANDAS
AND OTHER
MAMMALS AND BIRDS
SCALE</td></tr>
</table>

5 4 3 2 1 0 1 2 3 4 5 Miles
Elevations in feet

LEGEND

Populated place	Wen-chu-an
Camp	∧
Province road	—————
Expedition trek	– – – – –
Mountain peak	x17546
Concentrated habitat of Giant Pandas	⬭

Notes: Map compiled from various sources.
Contour intervals are in multiples of 330 and
660ft. Trek locations, camps and habitat area
plotted from Wm. G. Sheldon's Journal.
Map compiled and drawn by A. A. Gioiosa.

PEOPLES REPUBLIC
OF   Wen-chu-an
CHINA

More jabber. Fung: "Maybe yes, no."

Anne: "Just how is man sick? Can't he eat?"

Fung: "Don't know. Can't decide now."

After a conversation like this Anne generally gave some simple dietary instructions, for it would be impossible to tell what was or was not a proper medicine. Often men wanted medicine for a sick grandmother or some relative. A harmless pill of some sort was what everyone wanted, and they were never satisfied with mere directions and instructions.

Having eaten from at least thirty different dishes of delicious Chinese food, we sat around talking as we could through Mr. Fung. Most of our conversation was of a highly flattering kind. After a short time the magistrate announced he had irritating sores on both his ears and wished to have Anne treat them. Fortunately, we had ample light afforded by a kerosene lamp. We all gathered around with Anne and the magistrate in the center. I could not resist a smile at the naivete of the Wenchwan official and the ludicrous spectacle of Anne bathing his ears, endeavoring to make bandages and adhesive plaster stick to the sores. When the operation was complete, he was all smiles and seemed very thankful.

Our guests departed soon after the magistrate had been treated, and we spent some time repacking in preparation for our start to Tsaopo the next day. The coolies had carried about ninety pounds from Chengtu to Wenchwan, but for mountain trails we reduced the loads to seventy pounds. The mountain men all carried by back pack but we retained seven of our Chengtu men, who still seemed to prefer the bamboo cross pole.

We departed in mid-morning on September 17. To enhance our traveling we alloted tasks; Dean had charge of the food and cooking, Anne of the medical kit, Don the collecting boxes, and I kept a complete list of the contents of fifty different packs.

Crossing the bamboo bridge to the other side of the Min was a perilous adventure. The bridge was made of six cables of woven bamboo and reeds, each cable being about 2½ inches thick; these were fastened to stone piers on either side of the river. The cables were strung in two groups of three, about four feet apart, so it was impossible to cross from one side of the bridge to the other. A couple more cables strung shoulder high on either side made handrails with which to steady oneself. Occasional wooden bars tied crosswise underneath the foot-cables lent slight support to the whole rickety structure, which wobbled dangerously. The ends of the bridge crossed twenty feet above the water but in the middle it sagged to within three feet of it.

One had to keep a strong hold of the handrail at this point since the Min River was boiling below in a series of heavy rapids where it

The Sages on a precarious bamboo bridge crossing the Min River at Wenchwan

would have been disastrous to slip off. The only way we could cross
was to grip the handrails and walk on the firmest looking cables underfoot hedging sideways across the bridge. Interest was maintained by the fact that the cables kept rolling and slipping under one's feet; there was always the possibility of suddenly plunging down into the stream. Diversion came when you met someone travelling on the same cable you were, in the opposite direction. This necessitated a complicated flank maneuver not unattended by perils.

After crossing the river we began to ascend diagonally up the mountain slope, climbing higher and higher above the river. This was a real trail in the true sense of the word; it was narrow and steep and in many places there had been washouts and slides, making the way slippery and difficult. All the coolies wore straw sandals which adhered for a time to the muddy path. My sneakers had little traction in the wetter spots.

It gave me great satisfaction to be high above the Min and look from above at the gorges we had passed a few days since; we were soon up at a level with the clouds of mist which we had seen from below clinging to the top during the day. Although not actually on the summits of the ridges we were close enough to see that at least there was a limit to the cultivation of the hill. The crest appeared heavily clothed in trees and shrubs. Even at two thousand feet above the river bottom, on a slope so steep you looked down over cliffs at a sixty-degree angle to the stream below, every possible acre of earth seemed planted with corn. Fields of buckwheat and beautiful pink blossoms presented an appearance of so many light red blankets spread over the hillside.

We stopped for lunch at a medicinal root-picker's house on the steep side of the mountain. The owner was not at home and it took a great deal of persuasion on the part of our hunter, Kao, to gain admittance from the keeper. The latter at first believed we were soldiers attempting to break in.

In the middle of the afternoon we passed over the crest of a shoulder, dropped down across a steep ravine and climbed a few miles around the next promontory to a small hamlet nestled high against the ridge. The stone tower of a small castle was the most striking feature of the settlement. Large cedars grew around this village, where we passed the night. Some insect, the identity of which we have yet to determine, bit us all night making our beds rather uncomfortable.

The next day brought with it our first view of the mouth of the giant panda country we had been seeking for so many months, and it beckoned us to push on. It almost seemed like a dream. Weeks of preparation, more weeks of traveling, exasperating delays, all were forgotten. It is always difficult to realize one has reached a destination selected months ago in a place half-way around the world. At last we were at the portals of the best wildlife country in western China.

When we arose in the morning we were met by a native hunter named Wong. He had accompanied the Dolan expedition in 1931 and had been Ernst Schäfer's hunter. Schäfer had recommended him highly, and we made immediate arrangements to hire him. He proved to be probably the most valuable man we had. At six feet two inches he was taller than most other natives.

We ascended still higher in the early morning mist and the view up the Min River was most striking as the ever changing clouds of mist drifted in feathery banners along the slopes and summits of the virgin ridges.

Two hours after starting we came to the crest of a mountain where the trail descends to the Tsaopo Valley. It was from this vantage point we gained our first sight of the panda country. My feeling of elation and joy was unbounded. We saw the gorges of the Chengo River to the northwest where Dolan had found pandas. A few snow-covered peaks were dimly visible. The Tsaopo Valley lay to the southwest with its heavily wooded hills and was more virgin in its appearance than any country I had yet seen in China. It was too cloudy to see the high peaks of the sheep country two days' travel beyond.

The descending trail was extremely wet and steep for one wearing rubber-soled shoes. The others had straw sandals but I still wore my sneakers. It was muddy and slippery, and very treacherous to the unwary. We slithered down to the river bottom, crossed a little above the fork of the stream where the river from Chengwei comes in and an hour and a half of walking brought us to the town of Tsaopo.

We had been granted the use of Tso Tousa's castle here to live in and make our base for supplies. It seemed strange to find a castle in such a small village so far from civilization but the name was not misapplied. It was featured by stone turrets, walls, and very dirty spacious rooms. There was a smaller castle further up the hill. These were built by the Ch'iang people many years ago.

We found a large room for storage of our equipment and arranged for coolies to take us up to the sheep camp. Apparently the trail was steep and food scarce so a day was needed to recruit native men who were strong. They had to take most of their food with them.

We met another hunter who had a fox and a giant panda skin for sale; after lengthy bargaining we bought these.

We carried hundreds of Chinese dollars of silver alloy about the size of American silver dollars. These were also broken down in

Medicinal root porter, Min River Valley

Former palace and headquarters of the prince of Wassu in the town of Tsaopo, built about 1450 A.D., used as headquarters by the expedition

smaller denominations. Bargaining and paying the porters and hunters tested our patience throughout the trip.

Another native came in late in the afternoon with a young live blue sheep ram. Our hunter said there were flocks of hundreds where we were going. No doubt this was a gross exaggeration but judging from the number of sheepskin garments observed here they must have indeed been plentiful.

We invited the head man of the town, the keeper of the castle, and our hunter, Kao, to dinner. Western utensils proved more awkward in the hands of our guests than chopsticks in ours. Although we had planned to leave the next morning, a further day's delay was required for the coolies to gather the food they would have to carry up the mountain.

About 7:00 A.M. Dean, Don, and I set out down the valley with two hunters to search for goral in the narrow gorges below the peaks. This small goat with its short horns, dark brown body, and light tan stockings lives in the precipitous rocky brush-covered cliffs in the gorges of the stream and will venture deeper in the mountains if there are cliffs below timber.

Goral range widely in western China and, though probably local in their occurrence, are abundant in suitable terrain. The dense vegetation conceals them unless they are feeding or resting on an open ledge. As we were to find out later, they were preyed on by common leopards inhabiting the same type of country.

After getting a glimpse of one goral on the cliffs bordering the stream we found a sheer, precipitous cliff one thousand feet high. The men told us the goral (*shampan*) sleep on the ledges. Since we could see none Kao proposed to cross the stream, climb high above and roll rocks down in the hope of moving some. Although I had little confidence in such a method, there was little else to do during the heat of the day. I thought the best chance of seeing them would be in the late evening or early morning, when they should be feeding.

Two hours after Kao started we heard rocks falling and picked him out on the rim of a cliff high above us. With the first avalanche of rocks I spotted two goral bounding nimbly down along the cliffs. They were too far away and moving too rapidly to risk a shot. Two other goral were seen high on some ledges. No others were seen later in the evening.

We returned to the castle a little after dark and enjoyed a good supper. The magistrate sent us eggs, potatoes and a chicken as a gift for the meal we had given him the night before.

Ram and ewe blue sheep, or bharal

Chapter Four

The roof of the
giant panda world

WE started our ascent to sheep country in the morning, climbing directly up a tributary running in from the north. The stream was small and the hills closer together. I sensed at once that we were penetrating the mountains. Two miles above Tsaopo we followed a trail up the west fork and the climb up the stream bottom was truly delightful. It was the first place in China where I sensed an aura of wilderness. The complete denudation of trees in the more settled sections at lower altitudes had been very depressing. The stream was bordered by shady alder trees and willows, moss-covered rocks and many ferns contributing a pleasant aroma of freshness.

The path left the stream about a mile above the fork and ascended abruptly in a southwesterly direction away from the valley. It was not a well-used trail; instead of zigzagging it went straight up the steep grade. We climbed for about an hour and were well above the stream when, after passing through a corn-field, we came upon a farmer's house, where we decided to rest for lunch. This was the last farmhouse en route to the high mountain pass. Thus we were approaching the first entirely wild country I had encountered in China.

Only a few of our men had caught up with us an hour later so we decided to wait at least until our beds arrived. We were surprised and impatiently exasperated when they did not appear until 3:15 P.M. All the loads were not yet in. However, Dean decided we'd better go on with the tents, beds, and cooking outfits to make a camp two hours' travel beyond and proceed early the next day to locate a hunting camp site.

We started out and found the trail climbing up the mountain behind the farmhouse. After half an hour of walking it began to rain and Dean went far enough ahead to see that it would be useless to go on, for the route lay up to the crest of the ridge and there was only a slim chance of finding wood and water before dark. We left what loads we could and returned with the others to the farmhouse.

We made quarters in a room filled with corn husks and separated from the outside only by a thin latticework of bamboo. The usual pigs beyond the partition squealed and grunted most of the night.

Slipping constantly on the muddy trail up through the dense bamboos the next day, we were soon in the clouds of the upper reaches. With vision confined to a few yards we toiled up a very steep slope and became aware of why the porters had been reluctant the previous day to assault this mountain range—the Chiung Lai Shan.

The rate of travel was so slow that we were forced to camp on the ridge running up to the peaks above. We had ascended through the bamboos and entered the forest of gnarled, twisted rhododendron trees. I could imagine the appearance of these trees in the spring with the galaxy of colors—red, pink, and white.

After much axe-clearing we hewed out a small bench on the knife-like ridge, where we pitched a tent and managed to start a fire. Rain poured steadily all night.

Our objective was the *pei mu pungtze,* a medicinal root-picker's shack five miles further on. (The renowned botanist E. H. Wilson, who had collected hundreds of plants for the Arnold Aboretum in Boston before World War I, reported that the medicines sought by the Chinese are the bulbs of various species of *fritillaria* known as *pei mu.)*

After the usual confusion of breaking a camp in drenching mist we set off with renewed hope. As it was my responsibility to see that every man took his proper load I went on ahead of Don as soon as the last man had left. The trail led abruptly over cliffs, around rocky promontories, across rock slides, ever climbing to the pass at about fourteen thousand feet. The land above timber line is always a different world. In spite of the miserable weather I stepped above the last row of rhododendrons with great anticipation. Although the climb was treacherous. I began to look for wildlife signs, but it was not until the trail began to swing around the side of the mountain that I saw the first blue sheep track. This certainly gave me a particular thrill, even through the cloud blanket obscured surrounding high snow-capped ranges.

Near the pass on top of the range we saw a large fresh leopard track in the middle of the trail as well as the imprints of smaller cats. We flushed several beautiful monal pheasants from their rocky perches and watched them soaring out of sight into the fog below. Their favorite food are the same bulbs of *fritillaria* sought for medicine by the Chinese (Wilson).

At noon we reached the pass, where a crude stone altar set up on the top of the mountain marked the divide. The men insisted that a mile beyond was the long-sought medicinal root-picker's shelter where one could find wood and water. This seemed improbable to us as we knew we were close to fourteen thousand feet above sea level and timber line was some distance below. I went ahead of Anne and Dean and came upon very fresh tracks of a few sheep. Bamboo foot snares with birch sapling spring poles were set here and there along the trail.

What was my surprise, after descending over a thousand feet in the fog, to make out the crude roof of a shack just ahead of me exposed on an open shelf above timber line and enshrouded in mist. This proved to be the medicinal root-picker's abode and, although leaky and cold, it was large enough to house our coolies and most of our equipment. Enshrouded in mist it gave the impression of being suspended in the sky.

We pitched one tent and spent the next day pitching another tent and bringing up wood from timber line.

The first evening we spent some time bargaining with the coolies, and finished by keeping our Chengtu and Wenchwan men there and sending all but two of our Tsaopo men home, with the understanding we would send for them in two weeks.

When we awoke the next morning and stepped outside the tent I was fairly astonished by the sight before me. The valley was filled with mist, the sun was up and shining brilliantly on the peaks of the mountains west of us. Clouds would often obliterate the slopes while the summits pierced the heavens above or, drifting higher, banners of mist would cling to the peaks alone. At no one moment was the view entirely clear. The green of the slopes and jagged irregular array of peaks, precipitous cliffs, rhododendrons, and spruces leading down to the invisible abysses of the valleys below were visible at different times, suggesting to me the tremendous interest there would be in exploring these mountains on a clear day. We had hardly had an opportunity to survey the slopes with our binoculars before a sea of fog fairly boiled up from the valley bottom, completely obscuring the nearest peak.

We were to experience a great deal of fog at this camp; we were there from September 22 to October 14 and the only completely clear day was September 25 on our first successful search for sheep.

In the evening Don went to bed before supper as he was not feeling well, having a cold and indigestion.

The thermometer dropped ten degrees to just below freezing by dark and pouring rain changed to wet slushy snow. I stepped outside the tent at dawn and it was clear on the mountains. I aroused Dean, and, without waiting for any breakfast as we wished to take advantage of every moment of clear weather available, we both set out with our respective hunters, Wong with Dean and Kao with me. Dean started up the trail to the top of the mountain while I followed a trail beyond camp around the lower slopes of the range above us.

The fog swallowed me within an hour, and I saw one fresh sheep

*Suspended in clouds: blue sheep camp at about 11,500 feet. The
structure is a rootpicker's shack (Bei Mu Pungtze).*

track crossing the trail. Dean returned shortly after I reached camp and reported seeing a large fresh leopard track.

Our chief concern, however, was Don's physical condition. He seemed quite sick and had been in bed all day. The rest of us felt the effects of altitude to a minor degree, but we were not incapacitated. I spent part of the afternoon setting about three dozen small mammal traps in the hope of catching some specimens to keep me busy.

The reader may well wonder why anyone would collect mice or other small mammals. Not only is it important to know the classification and range of mammals in Asia, but they also play an important part in the ecology of the Szechwan mountains. Certain species are confined to different zones. For those not familiar with making study specimens for museums I shall briefly describe the process.

For each mammal caught measurements are made of the total length, the length of the tail, and the length of the hind foot, all important criteria in classification. The name of the collector, the date, the location including altitude, and the measurements are written on a tag to be attached to the mammal and entered separately in a field notebook. One cut in the skin of the abdomen area is sufficient to skin the small mammal, much like pulling a sweater off. the mouth is sewed, the skin is turned right side out, and the cavity filled with cotton and wire placed in each leg. They are pinned out and left to dry. The skull of each mammal is cleaned and preserved, since teeth may be the most important key to classification.

Carter, who was very experienced, could make up a skin in fifteen minutes. It took me about twenty minutes. Since sometimes we caught over forty mammals in one day it was necessary to train coolies how to prepare them. The task fell chiefly to Anne, who had been instructed in the method before leaving for China.

The basic prey in the alpine zone are the very abundant small mammals. We trapped 270 small mammals of ten species in the three weeks spent on the peaks. Eighty-four of these were shrews, including shrew moles, bi-colored shrews, Asiatic long-tailed shrews, striped-back shrews, long-tailed brown Shrews, and short-tailed shrews. The shrew moles are one of the mammal species confined to western Szechwan. Allen considered them very primitive and possibly forbears of both shrews and moles. Shrews are not ordinarily palatable to carnivores due possibly to the scent glands most species have so may not contribute to a food chain.

The soil must be productive of many kinds of invertebrate fauna to support such a large number of insectivores.

The shrew mole is confined to timber line or just below the rhododendron zone. Only two species, the long-tailed brown shrew and the bi-colored shrew were not caught at lower altitudes. Swan

(1961), in studying the ecology of the high Himalayas, found some species of spiders and other invertebrates high above timber line. He found many insects at sixteen thousand feet and one species of spider at more than twenty thousand feet. I have observed and caught shrews in shale and rocks high above timber line and vegetation in the Canadian Rockies. The only prey I could find on cursory inspection was a large species of spider. I suspect that some of the two species of Chinese shrews that I found confined to the alpine zone may well range higher than any other mammal, but since I did not go above fifteen thousand feet I was unable to verify this.

Three species of mice were found in this zone; the Asiatic wood Mouse was confined to timber line. We caught 141 voles from timber line to the highest peaks. The most abundant mammal was a short-tailed brown vole but a few long-tailed voles were also captured. One lagomorph, the pika, or mouse-hare, was largely confined to the high grasslands. Unlike the North American species these little hares were rarely found in talus and rock piles but ranged all over the grasslands.

The night of September 24 was warmer, and a rising moon created a magnificent picture. The snow-covered high peaks piercing the starlit sky reflected the white rays of the moon. The most impressive effect of all was the great lake of clouds below us—resembling the white early morning mist rising from a large lake. I sincerely hoped this would mean a clear day in the morning and would turn our luck.

September 25 was one of those days that will live forever in my memory. Before dawn Dean and I woke up to find the moon, still brightly shining, reflected by the floor of soft white clouds in the valley below. There was every hope of at least a few hours of clear weather.

We ate a hearty breakfast and discussed the respective routes we would follow. The hunters all insisted the sheep were on the top, so we decided to proceed together up the trail and separate at the crest of the range. We had hired three hunters, Kao, Wong, and Ho; the latter obviously wished to go, and, since I felt I only wanted one man, Dean said he would take him in addition to Wong so all five of us started on the trail up the mountain.

We had hardly traveled ten minutes before one of the hunters behind pulled my sleeve, muttering *"Panyan"* (the Chinese name for blue sheep or bharal). All three men pointed to the crest of the range two thousand feet above. Two rams stood on the sky line and passed quickly over a saddle just below a round craggy knoll of rim rock. With the aid of glasses several more were seen on the heavy black slope of broken rock just under the cliff. It was too far to be sure of the number or size of the sheep but we started to stalk them with keen anticipation.

Let me interrupt to describe the type of country we had to deal with and the environs, as this was my first opportunity to realize and not simply imagine the majesty and beauty of these ranges.

The first rays of a rising sun were lighting the clouds in the east, and the light was still dim enough to lend a lovely yellow glow to the moon. The tremendous bed of white soft clouds below reached up threatening fingers into the openings of the mountain ravines, but seemed as yet to promise sufficient time to execute a successful approach to the sheep. To the south, just peering above the fog was a low flat forested ridge and beyond were more ranges of dark high peaks. The impressive range opposite our camp stood out with more striking clarity than ever before, as there were no wisps of mist to envelop the precipitous gray rocky slopes above timber line.

As we climbed higher, still more distant peaks to the west with their jagged peaks and small glaciers towered above surrounding ranges.

The mountain we were toiling up differed a great deal from the range to the west. There were few sharp craggy peaks, and the highest point was probably close to fifteen thousand feet. There was a series of cliff-rimmed knolls with grass on the summits. The crest of the range was not razorlike but was more like a plateau broken up into innumerable pockets, ravines, and grassy basins. It was an easy terrain to ascend except for its steepness and wet slippery grass. One could surmount any of the craggy dome-shaped summits without difficulty. In the clear air at such an altitude distances are, of course, deceptive, and it required several hours to ascend from timber line to the crest, near as it appeared from below.

Amidst such inspiring surroundings and with the prospect of collecting one of the animals we most desired, it was little wonder that I felt great exhilaration, even in the face of a long tedious approach I knew to be before us. The sun was now shining full on the face of the mountain, and we paused to take some photographs of the panorama about us.

From our first position it was apparent the best method of reaching our quarry was to circle around the mountain and come upon the sheep from above. The detail of the route would depend on the movements of the animals and closer scrutiny of the land contours.

We continued on a trail passing through the mouth of an open ravine running up to the height of land. This appeared to be a good route as it would bring us up above the sheep and some distance behind them.

We paused a moment to rest, and Dean suddenly looked up at the crest ahead of us and whispered "There's a sheep." About four hundred and fifty yards above us and precisely where we intended to go, a large ram was striding across the slope. Then followed a sight such as no lover of wildlife will ever forget. Two hawks hovered around near the ram below the sky line. The *panyan* is the most strikingly colored member of his race. Bluish-gray in the body, black stripes on his legs, and the appearance of a black splash on his chest combine with the tremendous flare of his horns to offer a picture of wildlife hard to equal. Added to the mere physical beauty of this animal was his majestic carriage, as with head back he lifted his graceful forelegs high as he approached the sky line. In the early morning sunlight he paused between two rock-crowned pinnacles and, silhouetted against the sky, surveyed us. His every movement reminded me of our North American wild sheep, but he was even more striking in physical appearance.

He disappeared for a few moments behind one of the knolls only to reappear and watch us again before finally disappearing over the crest.

We became increasingly aware of the shortcomings of native hunters. They not only talked loudly but would not cease moving and pointing, thereby attracting the attention of the ram above. The hunters had superb eyesight and were excellent at following any kind of game spoor, but on the other hand, were excitable and apt to ruin a hunt by their impatience and overeagerness.

After seeing this ram we changed our route, and, instead of proceeding up the ravine, chose the rougher and more concealed approach of a bordering ridge of steep craggy grass-covered knolls rising successively, one upon the other, to a high pinnacle above. Three hours of climbing from the time we had spotted the band of rams brought us to a point overlooking the heavy talus where they last had been seen. We were keeping an eye open for the large lone ram, since we felt he was suspicious and would be very much on the alert. Were we to frighten him he might easily alarm the other sheep.

We tried in vain to make our hunters wait behind us, but no sooner had we gained a few hundred feet on them than they would arise and start following. It was at once obvious that we made a mistake to bring three men with us; as we learned later the best system was for one of us to go alone with one hunter, when it was easy to control him and there was no unnecessary conversation.

No animals could now be seen. It seemed probable they climbed around the projecting spur under us into a large basin invisible to us from our position. Proceeding on, always climbing, we finally arrived on the top of a grass-covered dome overlooking every possible hiding place of the sheep. From past experience with North American sheep I speculated the band would not move far, as it was near

Blue sheep terrain

the middle of the morning and they would probably be resting after their early morning feeding.

We had been searching in vain for several moments with our glasses on all the sun-flooded slopes in view, when I suddenly located the band in a shaded cliff-rimmed ravine directly across the mouth of the basin six hundred yards away. There were about a dozen rams, some standing idly on their feet leisurely feeding, while the others were lying down. They were in an excellent position for an approach since a level grassy saddle above their resting place was easily accessible without danger of being seen by them if we approached by a long secluded route.

We circled well around the basin, having to climb very high and further than we had anticipated. Far below us our tents appeared like white dots.

The men were coming behind, for we felt there was little danger of their frightening the sheep as we were well out of sight. Even so, it was extremely disturbing to have them with us as they were hard to control and continually showed a tendency to rush ahead. Wong, who had been trained by Ernst Schäfer, on Dolan's expedition, alone kept behind us. Occasionally we looked over from the crest of the ridge we were following to watch the sheep. Fog would now and then envelop them and would blow off again.

After half an hour of tramping we were reaching a point where we could make a favorable approach directly down the slope. We were just coming to a point overlooking a new section of sheep pastures when Ho and Kao, who were ahead, excitedly whispered "Panyan" and indicated that we should descend the slope a short distance to an open niche affording us a favorable view. There was just enough snow on the grass to make it very slippery, and, as we hurried down, I slipped and slid several feet before being stopped by Wong, who was below. Dean crept over the edge with his rifle, but a ewe in view two hundred yards away had already been alarmed by the hunters and dashed out of sight. This did not worry us a great deal as we were still some distance from the rams. We now concentrated on the final approach. By forceful gesticulations and signs we finally made the hunters wait, and we proceeded in suppressed excitement and suspense.

Little by little we moved down towards the grassy saddle, watching carefully and moving as quietly as possible. Having climbed five hours since we first saw the sheep we now only hoped the treacherous current of wind or unexpected movement on the part of the sheep would not spoil the day's work.

Finally we were both behind the final little rise separating us from the saddle, and we crept forward to look. A monal pheasant flew up suddenly uttering its loud alarm cry as it soared down over the cliff. This gave me a start for fear it might frighten the sheep.

I looked over a little before Dean and dropped back immediately as a ram was feeding in the saddle only twenty-five yards away. Neither of us were prepared for this, as we thought all the animals were still resting in the ravine.

We were just preparing for a shot when the ram possibly caught our scent, and before we knew it the entire band of twelve rams fairly stampeded in front of us, being in sight for a few brief seconds as they vaulted by the cliff and down the mountain.

We were in an unfortunate position for shooting as I was practically between Dean and the sheep and had to maneuver myself out of the line of fire. I shot once as they dashed behind the first cliff, but missed. As they reappeared, running down the cliffs about one hundred fifty yards away, I fired quickly again and saw one of the rams stagger and pitch over the cliff. They were far below when they came in view again and two hurried shots took no effect. Dean had crippled a large ram.

The hunters now came up, a few minutes after the sheep had disappeared below. They suddenly pointed over three hundred yards below and to our left, where some of the band was circling at the edge of the mist. I saw one short-horned sheep trotting in the mist at the edge of a ridge and took a long shot. I thought I saw her fall but all the others shook their heads. It was too far to be sure but I knew if I hit her it was a very lucky shot.

We descended immediately on the trail of the rams, hoping to find Dean's wounded ram. I saw my ram lying dead far below in the talus. We had not gone far before the hunters Wong and Kao picked up the trail of Dean's ram. I took Ho and climbed down to the carcass of my sheep to photograph and skin him. As we were taking the hide off a flock of snow pigeons wheeled by.

I was pleased to find a good mature ram, heavier than I had anticipated.

My reaction to the killing of this animal was not as elated as the prize might call for. The reason for this was principally that a long stalk with the possibility of securing a fine series of these sheep for the museum had been almost entirely spoiled at the last minute, and the final killing had not been clean cut but rather sloppy.

I found Ho to be excellent at skinning; his assistance was very helpful. After the skin was off I shouldered it with the head and my rifle while Ho carried the entire carcass.

I had been wearing straw sandals over moccasins all day and found them to be very slippery. Ho offered to take my load in addition to his; I let him have it for a short time but soon saw it was a very heavy load for one man, so by taking it back we were able to travel much faster. As we began to descend, we approached the rise where I had fired my shot at the sheep in the mist and what was my surprise to find an ewe killed by a shot I was sure I had missed. She was a poor specimen, with one horn much shorter than the other, but satisfactory for a museum. We cleaned her and I decided to send Ho back later in the day with a coolie to bring the body and carcass in.

As we hit the trail and started toward camp the joy of realizing that we had sheep meat and at least two specimens was marred chiefly by my worry over Don's condition and also by the possibility Dean had not found his ram, since I had heard no shot.

The first fear was completely annulled when I walked into camp to find Don up and skinning. He was weak but much better.

We were now all concerned about Dean until he walked in two hours later with a huge old ram, a true veteran who must have passed many years in the Chiung Lai Shan. The animal had been wounded and had descended almost to the valley bottom before Dean was able to collect him.

Between September 26 and October 7 the mist and fog, north winds and wet snow obliterated the mountains. We might as well have been living in a dense cloud. We could only work on small mammals.

On September 28 I made a significant find while tending mammal traps. I found the first droppings I had ever seen of a giant panda. A pile of cylindrical feces about four inches long and one and a half inches in diameter were found to contain nothing but remains of stalks and leaves of bamboos. This sign in the grasslands over one thousand feet above the nearest bamboo indicated that pandas occasionally wander above tree line. No bulbs or stalks of the rich flora above timber were contained in the droppings.

Native hunters brought in some pheasants caught by bamboo foot snares. The regal monal pheasant, about as large as a wild turkey, was seen often in flocks whenever we ventured to the peaks. Of iridescent bluish plumage it is an alpine bird I shall always associate with the mountain peaks of this area. When flushed it usually gave a whistlelike clarion call not unlike the warning cry of the marmots of our own Rocky Mountains.

The beautiful tragopan and blood pheasants were found at timber line, although blood pheasants were most abundant in bamboo jungles lower down. Other birds commonly seen above timber were ravens, a species of lark, flocks of snow pigeons, at least one species of soaring hawk (*Buteo*), sparrow hawks, and once I had a glimpse of a larger falcon I could not identify.

On another visit below camp I found a fresh takin track. The hunter Ho and I trailed it for two hours until it had broken into a trot and headed for timber below. The usual weather conditions precluded a sight of the animal. The owner of the root-picker's shack told me he had frequently seen takin above timber earlier in the year.

After supper one evening a runner arrived from Chengtu with a note from Mr. Dickinson informing us the Communists were making serious inroads into Szechwan Province and some fear was felt for the stability of the provincial government and safety of foreigners. He promised to keep us informed.

On October 6, descending from tending traps high on the mountain, Carter collapsed, suffering what appeared to be a slight heart attack. He had not been well ever since arriving at the high camp. We rigged up a chair from timbers of the shack the next day to carry him to a lower altitude. Sage and I, with four porters, helped to carry him up the steep trail to the pass. Accompanied by Mr. Fung and a cook he descended to Tsaopo, where he set up a very successful collecting station and quickly recovered his health.

The weather somewhat relented on our last four days in the mountains. After days encased in heavy clouds, I stepped out my tent door on October 8 before full daylight to a view that held me spellbound. In the north, across a valley below us, was a magnificent rugged range of high peaks cut by deep ravines with high basins holding small glaciers. The moon was still up, glowing deep yellow, as the rays of the rising sun cast a rosy light on the highest peaks piercing the clear sky as high as twenty thousand feet. Below was a great sea of clouds. In the deepest valleys I could see the distant spruces, the rhododendrons, and the bamboo slopes in the heart of the giant panda world.

I rushed through breakfast. As I set out with my Chinese hunter, Ho, banners of treacherous mist began to creep up the ravines near our camp. Proceeding up a rough trail east of the camp, I planned to leave this route on a prominent ridge where I would turn towards the peaks above and gain a view on two sides. Soon after starting, the fog enclosed us but kept lifting, giving some promise for a clear day at higher altitudes.

For the first hour we walked rapidly, arriving at the point where the trail crossed over the ridge. Ho wanted to cut back diagonally back over the slope above camp, but I insisted we keep to the ridge—a vantage point to see more territory. Thick snow began to fall fifteen minutes after turning up the ridge, but at the same time the mist lifted and all the glorious ranges around me suddenly sprang into view—peaks seldom seen from our camp, so all the more appreciated. Near the head of a large basin close to the crest above, I picked out about nine sheep almost a mile away. The best plan seemed to be to climb directly up the grassy ridge leading to a high hogback above. By following the top of this it appeared possible to gain the summit of a crag-rimmed knoll which would overlook the sheep.

Hardly had I visualized the approach when the clouds rolled in as dense as ever. We clambered up cliffs and steep grassy slopes, going from one saddle to another—ever climbing. Suddenly my eye caught a movement above me and I barely made out in the mist two sheep running upwards. One, a large ram, paused a few seconds on the sky line about seventy-five yards above me. He looked down at us, and I could only see his neck and head. I fired quickly offhand and fortunately killed him instantly. The other ram bounded out of sight. The dead animal rolled over and over down a ravine just below and parallel to the ridge. A shelf of broken rock stopped him just below us.

The mist lifted enough to allow me to photograph the animal—an old ram with heavy short horns. I measured him and left Ho to skin him and arrange to bring the meat into camp. As it was only 7:45 A.M. I took my rucksack and rifle and continued up the ridge to carry out my planned route. A flock of snow pigeons wheeled by me, disappearing into the fog.

As I ascended, the mist became lighter. I took off my hat to enjoy the warmth of the sun. This proved to be a mistake as it gave me a bad headache. We had all been thus affected at this altitude.

After climbing an hour I reached the crest of the mountain at about fifteen thousand feet; the sun was out in all its glory, and never in my life did I welcome it more. Constant rain, snow, and driving mist had been very cold.

It gave me the greatest pleasure and joy to wander alone along the crest of this shoulder. Many small and lovely blue gentians began to lift their withered and drooping heads from the cold grass and seek the invigorating rays of the sun.

The south side of the ridge where the sheep were was broken by a series of parallel spurs and shoulders furrowed by narrow ravines running down from the summit and abruptly falling off into rough cliffs near the foot of the slope. The north side dropped very precipitously in the steep sandstone ledges and rock walls, with narrow grass shelves, occasionally a small basin, and always a sprinkling of talus.

I did not tire all day of feasting my eyes on the very rough craggy range across the basin. Its highest peaks must be seventeen thousand feet and were magnificent as their rough outline was clearly silhouetted against the clear blue sky. To the southeast could be seen twenty thousand-foot peaks and ranges which barely projected through the white even floor of clouds—an inspiring sight and in view the entire day.

As I walked along the high crest I noticed particularly the large

Hunter Wong in blue sheep country

numbers of fresh sheep tracks. Other interesting signs were what I took to be the dung of foxes and also an occasional leopard track. Although the primary prey of these leopards was blue sheep, these cats probably preyed on monal pheasants and the large numbers of brown voles and pikas (mouse-hares).

A pair of ravens often flew overhead, while I observed one kestrel hawk.

Although it was clear on the top, the mist ceiling was but a few hundred feet below me and enshrouded the location of the sheep. When I arrived near where the band was last seen, the contour of the slope appeared entirely different from the shape we had seen from below, and clouds of fog concealed the sheep's exact position.

I chose a vantage point on a sharp spur above the approximate position of the sheep and sat down in the bright sun to enjoy a piece of chocolate and a pipe.

I had not been waiting long before I heard a fall of displaced shale just below the ceiling of the mist. I concluded that the band of sheep was moving down into the basin below, and it would be unwise to risk scaring them by attempting to follow them in the fog, which came and went intermittently, often affording me a view three hundred yards below but not far enough to see the sheep.

While searching with my glasses on the upper slopes of the magnificent range across from me, I spotted two ewes and a lamb a mile away walk onto a grassy promontory just above the edge of the mist not far below the high, jagged, irregular crest of the range.

After waiting a short time I descended the slope in the hope of seeing the sheep below the mist, provided I could approach closely without alarming them. I started slowly down and almost immediately found the fresh tracks of the band, which I began to follow cautiously. Every now and then I could detect the movement of the sheep by the sound of falling rocks.

I finally reached the top of a cliff overlooking the bottom of the basin, but the mist blinded me. I heard rocks falling on the opposite slope and so assumed the sheep had crossed over.

After waiting for two hours in the vain hope that the cloud would rise from below, I started back across the slopes toward camp, because I decided it was useless to stalk a band of sheep under such conditions, and there seemed no likelihood of their climbing above the ceiling of clouds.

About 3:30 P.M., only half an hour after leaving the head of the valley, the mist suddenly lifted, exposing the entire basin and opposite slope to my view. I hurried back to a more advantageous position and trained my glasses on the opposite steep slope. Almost immediately I spotted a band of nine sheep ascending high up near the crest, and a few seconds later I was astonished to pick out forty more sheep resting on a steep shale ravine above the basin. They were in a good position for a stalk, but it required at least two hours of steep climbing, and I doubted if I could ascend above them before dark. However, I determined to try.

No sooner had I made the decision and started the descent into the valley bottom than I was disgusted to see two native hunters climbing up the opposite edge of the mountain, obviously stalking the sheep. I climbed down rapidly in the hope of being able to ascend the face of the slope before the hunters had scared the sheep from above.

When I arrived on the valley floor, I paused a moment to watch the sheep, and suddenly a large ram arose and started down the rocky ravine toward the head of the basin. Almost immediately all the others followed. What interested me was to see rams, ewes, and lambs together in one band. Schäfer has recently told me he found both sexes in bands in May.

The sun was directly in my eyes as it began to set behind the high mountain above the sheep, and such a sight as I enjoyed during the next hour will never be forgotten.

I did not wish to change my position until I could determine the probable movements of the animals. Unhesitatingly they descended the slope, jumping from rock to rock until they had reached the floor at the head of the basin some five hundred yards away. At once they began to feed upwards on the range I had been on all day, and I realized that here lay the explanation for the many fresh tracks seen during the morning, for it was apparent they had been frequenting this basin for some weeks and during the early morning and evening fed on the more fertile slopes on the north side, while during the day sought the shelter of the rougher and steeper slope of the mountains on the south side.

There was no possible approach without great danger of detection except from above, requiring a reascent of the slope and a return to the head of the basin.

I immediately set out to do this and retraced my steps as rapidly as possible. When I believed I had attained sufficient altitude, I waited a few moments for the sun to drop behind the range, and I climbed along the slope in the gathering dusk from the head of one ravine to another, continually watching the basin below for the sheep.

At last, as I cautiously climbed over the crest of one of the last two spurs lying between me and the head of the basin, I looked down and saw the rear guard of the band feeding unalarmed in the grassy pockets among the broken rock about three hundred yards below.

Never shall I forget the beauty of this evening as I lay down to watch these sheep. The setting sun, for some time invisible, lighted the roof of the cloud ceiling far above to the southwest, tinting it with a fading pink and golden hue. The distant peaks, thrusting up twenty thousand feet through the belt of fog added tremendously to the effect. To have a band of fifty sheep below me contributed the perfect touch to make me feel the deep enjoyment of a wilderness of tremendous peaks, valleys, and distances.

I estimated roughly that fifteen minutes remained when I would still have light enough to shoot. A closer approach to the sheep might require at least this amount of time and probably more, so I decided to risk the success of a long afternoon's stalk by trying a long shot at a fine ram I had picked out below.

With rifle cocked I crawled forward and was about to take aim when my eye caught a movement on a spur about seventy-five yards above me. I glanced up to see one of the rarest sights in any wild country. A large fox, very bright red in color, bounded up the slope and turned around to survey me. I pondered a moment whether to spoil my whole afternoon's work by an attempt to collect him or to fire at the ram below. I chose the latter course, and as the events of the next few moments illustrated, my decision was probably not the wisest.

I slowly took aim and fired. I believe I shot over the ram; he seemed untouched and the entire band immediately dashed across the basin and up the opposite slope. I fired two more distant shots at the fleeing animals without effect.

As they ascended the opposite slope high up in the shadow of the great peak above, my heart sank a little as I realized the failure of the stalk and only regretted that another hour of daylight had not been available to permit a closer approach. At the same time, my disappointment was offset by the loveliness of the evening, the elation with which the sight of such wild game always fills me, and the magnificent panorama surrounding me.

Night was setting in rapidly, and I hurried down into the valley bottom. One last glance had revealed the sheep dimly visible far up the mountain, nervous, but resuming their evening meal.

The two hunters met me in the basin bottom, and we started back to camp. I was quite tired and especially thirsty, as I had found no water all day, testimony to the steepness of the terrain. I enjoyed a long drink in the brook flowing through the basin.

The return to camp was not pleasant after darkness overtook us and we had descended into the fog. It was so dark one had to feel with one's hands for footholds on the steep slopes, and it was a relief to be met about a mile from camp by the hunter Ho, with a flashlight.

I returned to camp two hours after dark to find Dean and Anne had had the misfortune to have missed a chance at a band of thirty-four sheep because of clouds of mist.

On October 11 we enjoyed one of the clearest mornings we had so far experienced. The Sages and I set off together in the company of Tso, a native hunter I had met up the valley while stalking the large band of sheep. As a man who spent most of his time living in the sheep country, we believed he might know, through constant observation, the ledges the sheep were accustomed to rest on during the day.

The fog hung lower in the valley than ever before so that for the first time since our arrival the details of the foliage on the lower slopes were visible. The general effect was that of great verdancy of various shades. Below the edge of the open grass slopes was the dark green foliage of the rhododendrons interspersed with an occasional spired spruce top; lower down was a scattering of deciduous trees including birches, maples, and various shrubs—many of them viburnums. I could detect bamboo growth at a somewhat lower altitude. There were few openings below timber line visible from the mountain but we were later to find open fields bordering bamboos near the valley bottom. I saw the contours of many very steep hills, and deep-cut ravines with projecting ledges and cliffs.

In contrast to the clarity of the lower slopes there was a heavy mist clinging to the top of the mountains. For the first time the weather conditions were exactly reversed and I was anxious to see how the day would turn out. When the sun rose I hoped the mist on the peaks would disappear.

As soon as it was light enough to walk we started on the trail above camp toward the basin. Bright golden tints on distant clouds to the east announced the rising sun, casting its rays on the sides of the slopes above.

We kept our eyes open all the time for sheep. As I was ahead I paused at the summit of each rise to survey the sides of the mountain unfolding before us. I did not expect to see sheep until we had reached the ridge where I had shot my last ram. When we arrived at the foot of this I hurried up to look over the crest; since the fog was beginning to roll up from the lower valley visibility was to be limited.

When I had ascended about half-way up the ridge I heard an exclamation from below, and looking around comprehended from the signals of the others that Tso had reported *panyan* up the ravine. I stopped immediately and, searching with the glasses in the direction indicated, picked out a band of eight sheep very close to where I had shot a ram. They were travelling rapidly upwards, disappearing into the mist. It was apparent that a stalk with so many people would be useless unless the mist lifted.

We continued up the trail and the fog became more and more dense until eventually we arrived on a spur projecting across the mouth of the basin where I hoped we would be on a route used by sheep. We waited for over an hour but the fog showed no signs of lifting for the day.

Our one remaining chance seemed to be that of a clear evening or early morning. To make the most of this Dean started back to camp to collect our sleeping bags, some tarpaulins, and a little food for the night.

Anne's knee had been very painful, and it had been at once obvious she could not return to camp and come up the same trail early the next morning in time to arrive at the basin shortly after daylight, when I felt we would have the best opportunity for a clear view. Our best chance was to spend the night there, while Anne could rest her knee the remainder of the day, in anticipation of a possible climb early the next day. As we waited several flocks of snow pigeons swept by us.

We had sought the shelter of a large rock in an inconspicuous place overlooking the bottom of the basin. I spent some time gathering what ground juniper I could find along the ledges to make beds. There were many fresh sheep tracks on the slopes above the basin. I didn't want to go far, as I wished to run no risk of scaring any sheep by coming upon them at close quarters in the fog and thus spoil our chances for tomorrow.

When I returned to the shelter of the rock we had chosen for the night's resting place, Dean was just coming with several coolies carrying our sleeping bags, some tarpaulins, ropes, extra clothes, and freshly cooked stew in a double boiler. In addition he had our primus stove, to be used not only for heating water and food but for warmth. Tso had gone back to camp, but Wong came up to spend the night, while the other coolies returned to the *pei mu pungtze.*

We all set to work to establish our night's quarters as comfortably as possible. With the aid of several crude poles Dean had brought, some stakes and ropes, we rigged up an eight-foot-square canvas tarpaulin as a lean-to, using slickers and empty duffle bags to keep the wind out of the sides. It was about four feet high in front but gave us shelter for the night. The ground was rough, but we levelled it up as much as possible with juniper boughs and over these put two air mattresses Dean had brought. We used the other tarpaulin for protection in front and just at dark crawled into our confined quarters, and Dean started the stove to heat up a pot of stew and made some hot cocoa. Wong crawled under the front tarpaulin and, with his two light blankets and sparse clothing, was appreciative of our company and shelter.

After some struggle in keeping the primus stove hot we enjoyed an ample meal of stew and hot cocoa. I wrote my day's journal by candlelight and prepared for bed.

Unfortunately the tarpaulin covering our heads had formerly been used for salting sheep hides and there were several spots where enough salt remained to collect moisture from outside and drip through. As it happened, one of the worst spots was just above my head. At my feet was Wong endeavoring to use the foot of my robe as a pillow. The necessity of drawing my feet up to avoid the latter and pulling down my head because of the former made for rather cramped quarters. However, I managed to get quite a lot of sleep as I am sure Anne and Dean did also. On the whole, considering the circumstances, we had quite comfortable accommodations.

Half an hour before dawn we were up and had started the primus stove to heat up the remainder of the stew and more hot cocoa for breakfast.

When the light was still dim the sky was very clear and our hopes for a clear day ran high. As usual, hardly had we finished breakfast when clouds blew up from the valley and obscured everything from view. It was still so early I felt there was yet a good chance for a break, but we took advantage of the unfavorable hunting conditions to break camp and leave packs for the coolies, who had been ordered to return about noon to carry them back.

In a few more minutes the clouds began to lift and I hurried with my glasses to the crest of a spur just behind us to survey the ridges below. The head of the basin was still enshrouded in mist. It gave me great pleasure to be up so high in the mountains at such an early hour. Awakening of life, what there was at such heights, was evident on all sides. Calls of the monal pheasant echoed across the ridges; the call of one of the common larks reminded me of a robin, while small flocks of rock buntings and an occasional one of snow pigeons flew past. I trained the glasses on the ridge where I had shot my ram as well as the visible part of the intervening slope.

I took the glasses down a second and Wong, who had just stepped up, said "Panyan," and pointed to the crest of the ridge, where a sheep had just stepped up on a sky line. I could make out with the glasses two others below.

We hastened to start toward these sheep as the mist blew in once more. I started ahead climbing diagonally up the slope. When the fog lifted again, the sheep were not in view. It was obvious they had gone over the crest. We hurried on in the hope of getting within range at the top of the ridge.

As we were clambering along the very steep side we heard voices below and could make out some of the coolies in addition to the hunter Ho coming up the valley. This irritated us considerably, as the men had disobeyed strict orders not to come for their loads until later in the day. I was walking ahead when the mist cleared again and had my eyes peeled on a point high up on the ridge that the sheep

had gone over. I heard an exclamation from behind and stopped immediately, looking carefully ahead. What was my surprise to see a band of sheep on the sky line, several hundred feet below us. They were about six hundred yards away standing alert, looking at us.

We all kept perfectly still, and, with the glasses, I distinguished nine sheep, all ewes with the exception of one old ram and one younger one. I knew they were not as yet badly alarmed but realized the sight of four people would make them uneasy. They started climbing and headed up the valley, crossing out of sight behind an intervening ridge. I believed they would cross the slope above us, and, from my observations of the last day I had hunted on this range, I guessed they would eventually go to the head of the basin to seek their daily resting place under the protection of the high ledges on the range south of us.

I regretted the four of us were together, as I felt Anne would have the best chance of securing sheep by hunting alone with Dean. Of course, we hoped all of us could approach a band, thus being able to secure a more complete series for the museum, but I knew that the chance of so many people hunting together would depend on an unusually favorable location of a band for a stealthy approach.

Dean started back a short distance and climbed directly up a steep ravine, all of us following. We had not climbed far before we saw another band of sheep passing over the sky line near the head of the basin. At the same moment my eye caught a motion below. Ahead of us we saw yet another band passing over the cliffs to the bottom of the basin not far above our night's camp; they crossed over and climbed into the mist on the high cliffs opposite us. These animals had certainly been alarmed either by our scent or that of the coolies far below. Mist kept blowing in, providing us with favorable opportunities to ascend the open slopes and not be seen by the sheep above.

A little farther up we saw the first band of the morning moving high across the ridge above us and a fourth band feeding quietly in the head of a ravine parallel to us. The mist closed in again and, strange to say, no more sheep were seen that day. We climbed on to the top of the range, to at least fourteen thousand feet. Anne deserved great credit for making such a long, steep ascent on a bad leg. When we arrived at the summit, it cleared as I had not seen it since that rare day of September 25 when Dean and I secured our first rams. For the first time the details of the mountains around me were entirely open to view and I have seldom seen a more magnificent mountain panorama.

Looking below on the southeast side, the cliffs dropped off precipitously to slopes of talus and beautiful green grassy slopes and basins. I was surprised not to see any sheep. Great cliffs of sedimentary rock as well as sandstone and some limestone made up the greater part of the formations, while here and there was a quartz or granite infusion.

At our vantage point we were very close to the highest point of the immediate range, although the great craggy mountains to the southwest which harbored sheep on their lowest slopes must rise to over sixteen thousand feet.

Distant ranges were not as clear as one could wish but enough were in view to give the impression of an endless sea, with peaks shining above the fog resembling islands. This galaxy of mountains was always awe inspiring.

We searched every available hiding place for sheep but it was obvious that all had retired to the shelter of the steep ravines and ledges across the basin. Mist kept blowing in, never allowing an entirely clear view across the basin. However an occasional shower of displaced talus convinced us the sheep were there.

We began the descent toward the path at the head of the basin and paused for a few moments on hearing more falling rocks, but the fog blew in denser than ever; even if we had sighted the sheep they probably would have been too high to execute a stalk. I wanted very much to wait until evening on the chance of getting them when they descended to feed, but we decided to return to camp. This was our last day in the high mountains. I regretted that such poor weather had precluded interpretive observations of sheep.

Most of the large mammals of western China have not been studied in detail, although at the time of writing Dr. George Schaller, employed by the New York Zoological Society, is making a thorough study of blue sheep in western Tibet and has published a preliminary paper on the behavior of these animals. Behavior is often the key to proper classification of different species.

Blue sheep are morphologically similar to both sheep (*Ovis*) and true goats (*Capra*). Allen has suggested such species as the blue sheep may have been progenitors of both sheep and goats.

Without going into anatomical details, blue sheep are allied to true sheep by general appearance, horn formation of the females, lack of a beard and presence of scent glands on their feet. Their massive skulls are goatlike; the horns of males resemble typical goat horns, and like goats they have markings on the anterior surface of their legs, have large dew claws and their tail is bare underneath. Schaller states the blue sheep is generally considered to be an aberrant goat with sheeplike affinities.

As I have already shown, the sexes are not necessarily segregated. We saw flocks of both sexes and all age classes. True sheep, except for the breeding season, are usually segregated by sex in different flocks and often somewhat different types of range. Schaller found the rutting season was late in the fall, usually in December. Therefore we were in the mountains two months before the usual breeding season.

Schaller's detailed studies on blue sheep behavior have led him to conclude that they resemble goats in their behavior: in postures, various forms of aggression, and methods of clashing of horns.

The common leopard in Szechwan and the snow leopard in Tibet are the chief predators of blue sheep. There are wolves in Tibet and wild red dogs in Szechwan as potential predators, although sheep seek high craggy inaccessible refuge when pursued by any of the canine family.

I could never understand why the sheep we saw were so wild. Once they detected us they bolted for several hundred yards, not tarrying to look back as most Rocky Mountain or Northern Dall sheep are inclined to do. The logical conclusion would be that man is the chief predator but I found even this difficult to believe, because the only weapons I saw were crude matchlocks shooting a type of grape shot and obviously only effective at very close range. Many young sheep are caught in foot snares—a hazard which may have resulted in wildness.

In the area we investigated sheep commonly left high craggy ledges at sixteen thousand feet and crossed a mountain valley, climbing to the range where we camped. They fed from about eleven thousand feet to fifteen thousand feet. Although there was some rim rock, a few ledges, and some talus it was a terrain characterized by grassy knolls, with scattered ravines. Grass covered ninety per cent of the surface.

The botanist E. H. Wilson has vividly described the carpets of bright flowers in the alpine zone in summer. They include primroses, gentians, orchids, *Spiraea,* many composites, and dwarf juniper. He found seventy species of fumeworts, thousands of louseworts comprising over one hundred species, and many species of ragworts. There are various nutritious grasses everywhere.

We packed up on October 14 and returned to Tsaopo, where we found Carter busy preparing mammals and birds. Tsaopo at four thousand feet above sea level represented a different life zone from other collecting camps, and many of the mammals he had obtained differed from the species of higher altitudes. He had trapped two new kinds of Asian wood-mice, two new shrews, a rock squirrel, and one wild rat. The fifty birds he obtained included the white-capped redstart, tragopan, Chinese crow, blood pheasant, spangled drongo, yellow wagtail, koklass pheasant, buzzard, kite, lesser spotted eagle, sparrowhawk, black-headed shrike, and ruddy turtle dove. The crows, hawks, wagtails, and redstarts were the most abundant.

Don looked considerably better than when he had left the mountains, and we were all much relieved.

Just before supper on the night of October 16 some excitement was aroused by the appearance of a bat flying in the castle rooms. After a long chase with flashlights Don and I finally had him cornered in a small room in the back of the house and Don took him off the wall so a new genus was added to our collection.

On the second day, Floyd Smith, the animal collector for the Field Museum of Chicago, arrived from Chengtu with a package of mail. Smith was on his way north and had simply come up here to see his representative in Tsaopo. He had trained men all along the range in collecting the mammals and birds and had taken out over ten thousand specimens from these mountains. He came to supper, and we enjoyed a delightful evening of conversation. He told us a great deal about the country for he had been collecting there for a number of years. He had covered such a wide territory that his only way of getting complete collections had been to train men at different places; for the most part he had travelled the main valleys and not penetrated the high mountains.

We had planned to rise early in the morning to go hunting for goral but decided to postpone it for a day due to Smith's arrival and an invitation from his representative in town to join him for a Chinese breakfast.

The name of Smith's agent there was Liao and we all assembled at his house about 8:00 A.M. for breakfast. The meal proved to be ample and delicious, although a little too rich for my palate. Sugared walnuts growing abundantly in this section now, fried pork, boiled chicken, cooked fungus and vegetables, minced meat and pepper, Chinese wine and tea comprised a few of the ingredients on the table. I certainly ate to my capacity in order to satisfy an appetite whetted by my days on the mountains.

The day was the clearest we had enjoyed for a month. The sun was out all day and it was cool and lovely. I took advantage of the weather to go out with Smith in the morning to take several photographs of the castle from several points. Smith informed me that it was reported to be five hundred years old, and at one time was the headquarters of the princes of Wassu. These were people of the Ch'iang tribe.

We spent the next day goral hunting, planning to leave for the heart of the giant panda range the following day. At 4:30 A.M. we rose for an early breakfast. Smith planned to leave with his men for Wenchwan, while I intended to go with Anne down to the gorges where we had seen goral before. Anne had a chair to go down the valley, having made the wise decision of saving her knee as much as possible. She hoped to spot a goral across the gorge in the first hour or two after we arrived.

I hurried on ahead in order to reach the upper cut of the gorge as early as possible. I arrived forty minutes after daybreak and, choosing a vantage point, scanned the opposite cliff very thoroughly. I was surprised not to pick up a goral as they would certainly be feeding at this time.

Anne caught up twenty minutes later, and we spent the next hour watching the cliffs around the head of the gorge and a few hundred yards downstream. Not a single animal was seen. Anne decided to return, while I proceeded down the stream, intending to cross the river and climb the cliffs on the other side. Fog was drifting in and hanging to the summits of the ridges but did not drop low enough in the gorges to interfere with any search.

I followed the trail rapidly, pausing once in a while to survey all the cliffs in view, but no goral was to be seen. I observed two lizards along the edge of the trail and birds of smaller species were abundant in the river bottom; among them I recognized a plumbeus water redstart we had been collecting. Sparrows were plentiful, while occasionally I saw a flock of the striking ruddy turtle dove.

I crossed the stream by tying myself to a bamboo ring on a single bamboo cable and shinning across.

Once across, I immediately began to climb the cliffs above. It was not high and the route up was not very rough as I had picked out from below a route up a good-looking grassy ravine. Once I had attained the elevation I wished I started across the slope horizontally, encountering extremely rough and difficult traveling. The going was over a steep side slope made up of treacherous bush-covered ledges and impenetrable high bushes. To add to the difficulties I encountered at least five kinds of common bushes which were covered with thorns, among them rose, prickly pear, and sallow thorn. Most of the time I could not see more than fifteen feet in any direction. I had to swing my rifle on my back to use both my hands to cling to the bushes and pull myself over the cliffs. In many places I had to push my rifle ahead and crawl on hands and knees.

I followed goral trails as much as possible and found quantities of fresh tracks and dung. In one place I saw a leopard track. It was easy to see how the goral escaped detection from below, as the trails led up ravines overgrown with shrubs that were ten feet high and very dense.

I struggled on for three hours and found my only chance of finding goral was when climbing over the crest of a ridge and examining the ravine and spur beyond.

About 2:30 P.M. I started down, intending to go back, when I happened to glance behind and see a goral a little over two hundred yards away at the top of a cliff, just below where I had come an hour or so before. He was facing me and offered a small mark but I found a good resting place and taking careful aim, fired. The animal seemed to half bound and half fall down the cliff in my direction and almost immediately disappeared in the high brush. Unfortunately the going was so steep and so rough it took me over an hour to reach the ravine where he had disappeared and I could find no sign of him. I could not be sure it was the exact location but searched as carefully as possible. This was the only animal I saw all day.

As it was getting late I hurried down over the cliffs to the river bottom. In several places I had to let myself down over the steep ledges by holding onto the bushes and I believe it was fortunate they held as securely as they did.

I hit the valley a mile above the bridge and had to descend to the bank of the river to reach it. I decided not to wait to tie on the wooden ring a native had left, and, with my gun and rucksack, decided to climb across on the bamboo rope. The opposite bank was a good deal higher than the one I was on. Half-way across I knew I could not make it. I started back to the other side. Of course I was faced the wrong way and it was by the greatest effort that I managed to get past the swift current and drop into three feet of quiet water by the bank. It was with some relief and the loss of my watch that I clambered back onto the bank and tied on the wooden ring.

Once across I hurried back to Tsaopo five miles upstream and reached the castle an hour after dark.

Takin

Chapter Five

Off for the giant panda valley

O N October 20 we arose early in preparation for a prompt departure but the coolies did not come at daybreak as we had anticipated so the last load did not finally leave until about 9:00 A.M. Our route for Chengwei lay, for the first stretch north from Tsaopo, up the same tributary we had followed to our sheep camp in the Chiung Lai Shan. We pursued this for three miles above the first fork. Instead of taking the trail up the west branch we followed another that climbed up on the ridge northwest between two streams. Alders, willows, and some poplars grew on the banks of the stream.

Anne traveled on a chair, while Dean and I followed behind. Don stayed in Tsaopo for a few more days collecting and would join us later.

Wong had brought his dog, Habor, a more intelligent-looking beast than most of the dogs I had seen in this region. The color and texture of his hair resembled a German shepherd but his tail curled over his back. Wong led him all day on a chain.

We stopped at Ho's house a few hundred feet above the fork and went in while he packed his bedding and clothes for the trip. Outside his house there were some men fashioning a wooden bowl. They used a narrow axe and crosscut saw skilfully. His house was constructed with walls of stone slabs and a roof of soft wood shingles. It was dark inside and fairly warm. Numerous paper pictures of Chinese heroes and idols adorned the walls, while at one end was a small altar with incense sticks. There were many children of all ages. Ho's wife was a fine-looking woman with strikingly handsome features so typical of many of these mountain women. Corn, pumpkins, and squash were hanging up inside while outside were high racks of beans drying. Several swarms of bees made their hives in specially constructed cylindrical kegs. Pigs and chickens ran loose outside as well as two mangy dogs. This small farm was similar to others I was to see in the mountains.

As we climbed higher it was apparent we were in a pasture country. Tracks of cattle as well as the animals themselves were in abundance all over the hillside. Grass was luxuriant, interspersed with many high bushes and trees of the poplar and maple families.

Their leaves were changing to shades of yellow and red and were indeed beautiful. To add to the color of the landscape were viburnum bushes laden with red berries of two varieties, neither edible according to the natives. There were thorny rose and sallow bushes, sumac, Chinese chestnut and bamboos higher up.

Crows circled overhead in abundance and I saw a sparrowhawk up near the edge of the mist perched on the crest of one of the small ridges. Great titmice were calling.

The tracks and rootings of wild boar became more plentiful as we ascended, while I was interested to see many runways of moles in the ground. We observed no wild mammal of any kind all day. The varieties of vegetation, the colors of the leaves, the frequent occurrence of fresh springs on the ground made the climb a delightful and interesting one, reminding me more of our pastureland in New England than any of this farm region I had yet seen.

Once up on the ridge we could look down across the valley to the farmhouse on the trail to Chiung Lai Shan. The crest of the mountain behind was as usual obscured by fog.

The greatest find of the day was some luxuriant patches of wild blackberries, which were very sweet and resembled our own in flavor. The bush on which they grow was thornless and had very large leaves. Dean and I picked two hatfuls in a short time and gorged ourselves on the sweet fruit. In the afternoon we penetrated the first stretch of bamboo and not far beyond we camped on a grassy bench on a hill with a spring flowing through it and plenty of wood on both sides.

According to Dean's altimeter we had climbed a little over four thousand feet from Tsaopo and our altitude was about eighty-seven hundred feet.

Rain poured all night but ceased soon after daylight.

The trail from our camp climbed steadily to the crest of a ridge at an altitude of ninety-six hundred feet. We had not ascended very far before the rain-soaked soil was replaced by a soft blanket of wet snow. Three inches covered the ground at the highest altitude we reached. It was truly a beautiful sight. Passing above the bamboo and grass slopes we penetrated a rhododendron belt where the trees did not grow too densely and were interspersed with large spruces festooned with hanging grey moss and whose broad boughs held aloft what snow had fallen. Occasional meadowlike clearings made walking relatively easy. Once over the divide, the trail descended rapidly and after dropping one thousand feet we passed out of the snow belt into a thicket of bamboo.

I proceeded in advance of Anne and Dean down through the bamboos and in a short time I was below the fog and could survey the country about me. Looking almost due west I could see up the tributary flowing into Chengwei, one of the best areas of the giant panda country, and the sight was one of great beauty. The most striking feature of all was the rich autumnal colors on the lower slopes. The bright yellow, red, and deep orange leaves of the maples, poplars, birches, and viburnums washed the valleys and slopes with brilliant color. Our eyes never ceased feasting on this galaxy of colors for several weeks before winter. The beauty of these hardwood leaves was in sharp contrast to the dark green coniferous trees, bamboos, and rhododendrons at higher altitudes. There were at least five kinds of evergreens including two kinds of spruces, silver fir, hemlock, and pine. Large poplars with broad leaves were very conspicuous. Blackberry bushes were common along the trail and we tarried to eat more of the fruit before reaching the valley floor.

After ascending another hill to an altitude of seventy-six hundred feet we arrived at the first farmer's house, where we stopped for lunch. We descended from the farmhouse toward the valley bottom headed for Tsapei, a group of farmhouses where we were to spend the night.

Arriving at the creek bottom, we followed the stream through beautiful narrow rock gorges fairly radiant with autumn coloring. Reaching the main tributary we went downstream about a half a mile and crossed to Tsapei, where at 3:00 P.M. we chose our night's quarters on the roof of a farmer's house. The altitude of this valley was sixty-two hundred feet. Later I was to find a panda visited this town.

The view from the roof of the farmhouse, especially as I saw it in the evening, was worthy of a brief description.

Noisily rushing below was a clear swift mountain stream bordered by clean steep grey cliffs cut over eons of time by the rushing water. There were colorful overhanging bushes of many kinds, including a few rhododendrons and willows. As I looked up the valley my eyes could distinguish deeper gorges ahead bordered by grey ledges overgrown with spruces and lit by the brilliant colors of autumn leaves.

Steep hills, rising three thousand feet above, completely surrounded us; these were the domain of giant panda and takin. The bright color of the leaves, mist clinging to the spruce-dotted tops, the bright coat of snow visible on their branches, the pines of the lower slopes and the open meadows added tremendously to the attraction of the panorama.

This region was the most hospitable and unspoiled section I had yet seen in China. There was fertility in the soil; the forests had not been laid waste by the wholesale cutting of trees; it was not barren and there seemed promise of tolerable weather. It was rich in its yields of small mammals and birds, and I felt much encouraged at the prospects for the next sixty days.

Arising soon after daylight, another fairly clear day dawned. We prepared to leave for Chengwei, composed of three farmhouses, where we intended to make our panda-hunting camp.

The small traps I set out the previous night yielded no moles but two kinds of wild rat, an Asiatic wood mouse, and an interesting new black vole, a species confined to lower altitudes.

We started up the Chengo River. We followed the south bank close to the water, except where a gorge required climbing above the stream. The colors of the autumn leaves were more striking than ever as we followed the path under overhanging limbs, through dark thickets of bamboo, and around moss-covered cliffs.

One of the most beautiful sights I have ever seen was a high waterfall spilling down over a high rock cliff into the rushing stream below. A sheet of spray flung out from the heights cast a mist over the colors of the foliage overgrowing the precipice.

Dean and I continued ahead of Anne and the coolies to cover the five miles to our destination. We wished to size up our new quarters before the coolies arrived. Two hours of walking from Tsapei brought us above the gorge of the small tributary flowing in from the south. The confluence of this stream and the Chengo River mark the location of Chengwei, which is merely the name of the fork and the three farmhouses above on the west side of the smallest stream. We made our way to one of these where Wong indicated that Dolan and Schäfer had stayed.

Looking up the tributary I was surprised at the large number of spruce trees on the steep ridges, and it is these that the giant panda is reputed to climb.

The next day was spent in camp arranging our permanent quarters for at least a two-week stay.

Before we proceeded with any of the day's work we called in the owner of the house, and with our cook, Jim, interpreting, we endeavored to find out what we could of the animals in the vicinity. He informed us that the *bei shung* (giant panda) might sometimes be seen just after daylight or at dusk on certain ridges surrounding his farm. He reported that he had seen none in trees except when chased by dogs. He had shot some using this method, he said. He stated that, with the exception of honey, their exclusive diet in that valley was bamboo.

As yet without any experience in securing pandas, I speculated on possible ways of finding them. First by trap, secondly by dogs treeing them, and thirdly by continuing to hunt them, with the chance of spotting one in a tree as the German Schäfer had succeeded in doing.

The next day was to be my first opportunity to find out something of the whereabouts and habits of the giant panda from first-hand observation.

The men reported that golden monkeys were found in the valley of the Mamogo, a day's travel from Chengwei.

During the morning Dean and I worked pitching another tent and by means of a bamboo framework rigged up a tarpaulin as protection for the long table at the end of the roof where we prepared specimens. I also used bamboo poles to construct a drying rack for mammal and bird skins. We cleaned up the room we had been using for eating, arranged the boxes in dry places and made a place for Don to stay when he came. It rained most of the day; at night a heavy wind came up and drove sheets of rain against our tents.

Bamboo jungle in the Chengwei Valley, with hardwoods on the valley floor

Chapter Six

The environment of
the giant panda

FROM our campsite on the roof of the farmhouse we could see giant panda habitat in all directions. The topography was awe inspiring. Precipitous slopes bordering the Chengo River and the Chengwei tributary rose so steeply that in places they appeared to run at an angle of seventy degrees. We found that the bamboo and spruce jungles concealed cliffs and ledges rising vertically and difficult to scale.

Looking due south up the Chengwei Valley the high snow-covered peaks of the Chiung Lai Shan range towered above the valley floor, often reflecting the last rays of sunset when the valley was almost dark. The valley bottom was at an elevation of about eight thousand feet. The sides were clothed in bamboo for at least three thousand feet of altitude, where the bamboos gave way to rhododendron forests at timber line.

We soon found that alpine bamboos were interspersed with many other types of shrubs or trees. Along the stream of the valley were a variety of hardwood trees, many with brilliant autumn foliage when we first arrived. Maples, willows, poplars, varnish trees, walnuts, and lindens grew at the lower altitude. Groves of beautiful white birches grew among bamboo jungles and scatterings of maples were common from the bottom of the valleys to at least one thousand feet above in the bamboos. Open fields surrounded by bamboos or bordered by bamboos were commonly found as much as two thousand feet above our camp. Shrubs in the openings and in any part of the jungle where light reached the forest floor were several kinds of viburnums, clematis vine, various species of wild roses, *Spiraea*, a type of sheep laurel, and many others.

The evergreens were very conspicuous. At lower altitudes there were various kinds of pines and larches. Schäfer shot a young panda from the branches of a larch tree only one thousand feet above camp and located in an open field. I found that a young panda had climbed a pine tree at about six thousand feet and surrounded by farmlands. There were at least five species of silver fir, as well as hemlocks and spruces. These grow on all the higher slopes to timber line.

In such a semitropical area at a latitude of thirty-one degrees it would require a separate treatise of many pages to catalogue the vegetation in giant panda habitat. Wilson, for example, found over one hundred species of rhododendron in western Chinese mountains.

In summary, giant panda habitat is not only characterized by the abundant bamboos but by the variety of other shrubs and trees and openings in the forest. To define the altitudinal range of the giant panda is to define the altitudinal range of bamboo, which can vary two to three thousand feet depending on exposure, rainfall and latitude. We found evidence of the giant pandas from fifty-five hundred feet above sea level to twelve thousand feet. A few wandering pandas at perimeters of bamboos would extend their occurrence higher and lower.

No description of this habitat would be adequate without some account of the fauna sharing the habitat.

Wild boar ranged from the Szechwan plain to the highest edge of bamboos, probably the most extensive range of any ungulate in China.

The bamboo jungle is shared by two unique goat-antelopes, the takin and the serow. The takin is a heavy, cattlelike beast weighing from six hundred to eight hundred pounds, with short powerful legs, short horns swept back like a gnu and a coat of almost golden color in Szechwan. Species of takin further west are almost a chocolate color. These animals are in panda country but not confined to it, ranging further west and southwest.

The serow is one of the commonest mammals in the bamboo forests and often frequents cliffs near the ridge tops. It is a large somber-colored goat with short horns and weighing from two hundred to two hundred fifty pounds.

There are a variety of small deer, from the diminutive musk deer weighing under fifty pounds to the muntjacs and tufted deer—all with short horns and inhabiting the bamboos. Besides the giant panda, large carnivores inhabiting the area are leopards, the Himalayan black bear, and the wild red dog. Little red pandas, a variety of species of cats, and fruit-eating martens are also found in these jungles.

Hugo Weigold reported a tiger was seen before 1913 in the Min River Valley at the perimeter of the panda range. Possibly at one time tigers inhabited the area but the natives did not appear familiar with them. There were more frequent accounts of tigers well south and southeast of the panda range.

We found golden monkey sign in December in heavy snow at 11,500 feet near a group of large spruces. Not much is known about this large monkey, but it is supposed to feed chiefly on bamboos.

The area was alive with small mammals. We caught 1,150 of these in the space of six weeks. It was not unusual to catch thirty or forty mammals from one hundred set traps. While trailing panda through the bamboos I often observed a network of small mammal tracks.

An intricate and colorful addition to the panda environment was the bird life, particularly the large flocks of blood pheasants, golden pheasants, and various species of brightly colored titmice. The most abundant groups of birds were three kinds of laughing thrushes, and two species of babblers and wagtails. Less abundant birds were four species of woodpeckers, the koklass pheasant, snipe, thrushes, wrens, chats, and several others (see Appendix Three).

This sketch of the environment is further expanded in the following narrative and in the last chapter.

Tufted deer, or "black muntjac"

Chapter Seven

Exploring the giant panda habitat

Tᴴᴇ day after camp was pitched we arose an hour before daylight and planned our first day in panda habitat. Dean was to hunt with Wong and his dog, Habor, on the west side of the tributary valley, below the farmhouse, while the owner of the house, Yan, agreed to go with me and Ho to show us the best place to set a panda trap—a location, I assumed, which would be a favorite haunt of the animal. Yan had lived in Chengwei all his life. Of indeterminate age, he was the senior citizen of this small settlement. He was one of two residents I met wearing a pigtail. He was a good woodsman and hunter and wise in his knowledge of the giant panda. He proved himself somewhat sly, often exaggerating difficulties and distances of travel, to avoid work.

Shortly after daylight we moved off in our respective directions. The owner of the house went ahead while I walked behind him, with Ho bringing up the rear. Our route took us up the valley about a half mile above the farmhouse to follow a ridge up on the east side. The weather was fair as we could see the sun on mountain peaks covered with snow at the head of the valley. The men said this was part of the Chiung Lai Shan range.

We crossed the Chengwei stream and started up a trail through the dense bamboo slopes. I saw the first droppings of the giant panda just above the river bottom. I observed a great deal of panda dung during the day and made a practice of picking apart samples. All I examined contained only bamboo.

Following a good game trail through the bamboos, the traveling was very steep but not difficult, but I could easily realize the difficulties of attempting to work one's way across the slope. I think not only Sage and I but others too may have overstressed the difficulty of traveling in these bamboo jungles. We were later to find it was extremely difficult to climb in a horizontal direction where there were a series of parallel ravines and ridges, but if one could confine travel to going up or down the slopes to the ridge tops there was usually a game trail. When we had climbed one thousand feet and were still in the dense bamboo we came upon very fresh droppings of panda, probably made within the last twenty-four hours. In such a damp climate it was difficult to estimate with accuracy the time such droppings were made. It was indeed encouraging to know that a *bei shung* was not a great distance away.

As we approached the end of a spruce-covered rocky spur projecting down through the bamboo forest we could observe many places where pandas had been feeding on bamboos of all sizes, torn off and eaten. They varied in diameter as measured by a steel tape from 1¼ to ¼ inch and some were bitten off as high as thirty-eight inches from ground level, although as we were to find later much higher stalks were pulled down and the leaves stripped off by feeding pandas. This did not uphold the reports of other authors that pandas eat only bamboo "shoots." According to Schäfer patches of shoots were favorite feeding areas in spring.

Once we had arrived at the first spruce trees the climbing became easier. The trail followed the crest of the ridge and the footing was secure. Here and there scattered bamboo thickets covering the ridge had to be passed and I found that this could be most easily accomplished by bending almost double or crawling on my hands and knees.

What interested me tremendously was the size and growth of coniferous trees of several varieties. Some of these were three or four feet through at the base but were stunted. They were not high, and the tops were covered with long, twisted limbs. The growth was suprisingly dense and did not permit any clear view of similar ridges on each side of me.

I had been told by Dolan and Schäfer of the "climbing trees" of the giant panda which were to be found on these ridges. I found several large ones with claw marks along the trunk certainly answering this description, but under none did I find any dung suggesting that any one animal or group were accustomed to climbing or resting in certain trees.

As we went along the ridge we saw two spear traps the house owner had used for killing pandas. Neither of them were set. The construction was simple and interesting; the principle was simply that of a heavy spruce sapling laid horizontally about two feet above the ground with its base bound to another tree. At right angles to the top was attached a strong piece of bamboo with an iron point securely fastened. Once set the point of the latter was just beside the trail; it took the strength of two men to pull the sapling back where it was set with a figure-four arrangement and a string across the trail; if tripped by an animal this very lethal spear would be released impaling an animal chest high. We later saw a large bull takin that had been killed by one of these spears.

When we had reached the second and last trap the house owner indicated it was not much use to climb any farther; as it was still early and I wished to learn something of the country I proceeded

Hunter Ho in rhododendron belt

ahead up the ridge with the two men following. The panda sign was still abundant and the well-beaten game trail facilitated traveling. We passed the base of a high cluster of tree-covered ledges and I observed that panda tracks had climbed up over these. I investigated and made the most interesting find of the day. In a sheltered dry depression under the cliff I found piles of panda droppings, giving unmistakable evidence of the resting places of the animal. None of the droppings were fresh, and due to the fact these "dens" were on the south side of the ridge I assumed they were used for shelter in cold weather. Bamboos had been torn off, forming a crude circular bed. I speculated how much easier it would be to hunt these animals in snow with the leaves off the trees. With good dogs or by means of effective traps they could certainly be more easily secured. Still, hunting was not wholly impractical, and I hoped for luck within the next ten days, but felt I would rather be entirely alone.

An hour's climb brought me well out of the bamboo belt and into the rhododendrons. Here I saw old takin and musk deer signs.

I had not gone far before I was at snow line and in the usual fog of the higher altitudes. It was raining and very chilly, and I had been quite thoroughly soaked climbing up through the bamboos. We rested for a light lunch of chocolate and corn-meal cakes. The mountain men of this area made corn-meal cakes as their staple diet. They would simply take cornmeal and moisten it thoroughly, making it into a round patty about three inches in diameter and one inch thick, then put it on the coals of a fire until it was hot all the way through. I started eating these and found them to be, although not very tasty, extremely nourishing, and I usually had a piece of chocolate to add to my midday diet.

We were almost on the top of the backbone of this particular ridge, having climbed up one of the ribs from the valley bottom. Here we hit an old logging road leading along the side of the mountain and down to the farmhouse. I decided to follow it back. In spite of such "logging" roads I found no area logged off and presumed occasional trees were cut to reinforce houses or fashion wood bowls.

I observed many new and interesting birds all day including a variety of titmice, several wagtails, and some bulbulls.

As I followed the wood road I ran across the first serow tracks I had seen. These tracks were very fresh and preceded me on the trail almost all the way down the mountain. The country along the side of the mountain at this altitude was quite open, with many birches, other hardwoods, and a few spruces.

The road descended abruptly. I could see where logs had been skidded down it from the top, making an almost straight trail down through the bamboos.

Not long after entering the bamboos we came upon very fresh

panda dung in large quantities. The men indicated they believed it to be the same animal we had seen signs of in the morning. They suggested that we take Wong's dog up next day to trail him. We were certainly willing to try this, but I wondered if the dog had a good enough nose to follow a trail over a day old, even in such damp country.

I paused again and again on the way down the slope to survey with my field-glasses the tree trunks and tops on the opposite slope across the valley but saw nothing. I returned to camp soon after this to find Anne had been directing five of the coolies skinning forty more mammals caught during the day. The majority of these were different kinds of wild rats, but there were four kinds of shrews, none of them new to our collection. This is the lowest altitude, seven thousand feet, where we caught the shrew mole and the highest for the long-tailed shrew. The latter seems confined mostly to lower altitudes.

Dean had found traveling very difficult on his side of the valley. He had seen a good deal of panda sign but none that was fresh and no evidence that the animals did more than travel through. Wong's dog had chased a serow and a muntjac, one of the species of deer in this area, and seemed to show ability at trailing. I hoped for success on the next day when we planned to put him on the trail of the panda on the slopes I had been on. Dean shot three striped squirrels, which are quite common both in the bamboos and, particularly, in the rhododendron belt.

It rained all night and was drizzling when we arose next day before dawn.

Our plan for that day was to take Wong, his dog, and the house owner up the trail I had descended the previous afternoon, in an attempt to pick up the trail of the panda whose sign I had discovered the day before.

As soon as we started the three dogs belonging to the house owner began to follow, and since he wished to take them we permitted it. I did not favor three unleashed dogs accompanying us, but decided to let the native hunt as he wished to give them a trial. Wong's dog was leashed.

No sooner had we reached the river bottom than the dogs started barking wildly on the trail of some animal. The men said "Cheetzu" (muntjac). We crossed the stream just in time to see a badger running under the bank with the dogs after him. I took a hasty shot with a rifle as he disappeared into the brush but obviously missed. Apparently he entered a hole, as the dogs ceased barking and followed us on the trail up the mountain.

We struggled up until we reached the panda sign about an hour and a half's ascent from the valley bottom. We were just on an edge of a wet belt of thin snow. We unleashed Habor, Wong's dog. It was apparent at once that the trail held little scent, and the dogs only puttered around in the bamboos a short distance away and showed no signs of excitement.

We descended the trail for a few hundred feet and decided to cut across the slope to the next ridge. I quote Sage's description of this route:

> We decided to strike across the mountain side to the spruce ridge we had seen from below, and which was separated from the ridge we were on by two deep gulleys and an intervening shoulder. Leaving the trail, we plunged into the wet bamboos and entered upon the toughest piece of going I have ever run up against. Clinging precariously to a precipitous grade we literally clawed our way inch by inch through a tangled mass of bamboos, thorns, trailing vines and creepers that caught hold of our feet, our rifles, our heads and in short, everything that could be caught hold of and tripped or snarled up. The bamboos grew only a few inches apart, and they grew in every direction but upside down, so that we had to alternately push them apart to crawl under them or climb over them. Sometimes it seemed as if we were doing all three at the same time. Cliffs and ledges covered with treacherous loose moss, where a slip would mean a dangerous fall, did not add to the security of our progress. Still, there was no question that this was the typical haunt of the giant panda, and it was easy to understand why hunting them was so exceedingly difficult.

As we approached the top of the spruce ridge the dogs began barking ahead and the men said *"Bei shung."* We hurried on as best we could, but as soon as we had topped the next ridge, all barking had ceased and the hunters shook their heads as the dogs returned one by one. Apparently it had not been a panda for at that time I thought such an animal would be easy for the dogs to trail. Later experience, however, indicated that this could have conceivably been a giant panda.

We climbed up a group of ledges and discovered a perfectly sheltered panda den which was just large enough for a man to crawl in and curl up under the shelter of a projecting rock.

We continued on crossing from one ravine to the next through the roughest forest of bamboos we had as yet experienced—thrash, thrash, thrash all the time.

In the afternoon we were relieved to finally strike the trail on the same ridge I had investigated the day before. As it was cold and raw we descended rapidly to the valley bottom.

During the day we identified four fresh heaps of panda droppings at different points along the slopes composed exclusively of bamboo leaves practically undigested with none of the stalks one can observe in many of the older signs. At the time we were baffled to explain this slight change of diet. Zoo studies give a clue. Morris found that female pandas in heat often ate much lighter food, preferring leaves, for example, to bamboo stalks. Brocklehurst claims that droppings composed of leaves were made by females but does not explain how he could have possibly known this.

My forebodings about the hunting ability of these native dogs was fairly well confirmed. They do not have the keen noses of a hound and must find a hot trail to be effective. One must hunt right with them as their range is only a few hundred feet. Also, they will give chase to anything with four legs so the best plan for panda hunting is to keep them on a leash until a fresh panda track is found or letting them range in an area where there is a great deal of panda sign.

A few minutes after writing my journal that evening I stepped out on the roof of the house and was astonished by the sight before me. For the first time since our arrival the heavens were clear and the tremendous peaks of the Chiung Lai Shan could be seen at the head of the valley, peaks reflecting the dim rays of the moon lighting the clouds in the east. It was typical of this country that our first view of these magnificent ranges should be at night, and they appeared unreal and phantomlike, their ghostly forms lighted only by rays of a moon so far invisible to us. It looked auspicious for a clear day.

Next morning the mountains at the head of the valley reflected the rays of the rising sun in all their glory. Standing out in perfect clarity was an array of lofty peaks piercing the brilliant blue sky. Fingerlike ridges clothed in spruces or rhododendrons stretch up above snow line to the great white slopes of the grasslands. The majesty of the distant view was tremendously enhanced by the foreground setting, a valley resplendent with various colors of autumn foliage, the brilliant hues of red and pink of the maples and the yellow colors of the silver birches, willows, and poplars.

We had decided to investigate the slopes up one of the tributary valleys of the Chengo to become more familiar with the range of the giant panda in this region. Yan, the house owner, told us a good trail led up the west slopes of the Chengo Valley. Dean and I were to explore this together, hoping to find high vantage points to size up the surrounding country with binoculars and thus more accurately speculate on the most favorable panda grounds.

Following a trail diagonally across the farmlands, we passed the third farmhouse in this group in the southwest corner. Here we continued on what appeared to be an old wood road with crude bridges and corduroy in soft places. Ever climbing, we passed over an open shoulder still below bamboos and covered in places by a few birches, maples, and low bushes. The rays of a warm sun were welcome in a land so constantly drenched with fog and rain.

After crossing the first steep ravine we entered an open parklike belt of spruces far less stunted than any we had so far observed. As we toiled up we reached freshly fallen snow, fortuitous for finding tracks. The traveling was so easy on this road we could move slowly and quietly as we traversed relatively open country increasing our range of vision.

After two hours of ascent we reached an open field commanding a fine view of the spruce ridges across the valley and the bamboo slopes I had hunted the two previous days. We searched the opposite slopes hoping in vain to spot a panda sunning himself on the branches of any of the trees.

After further experience I have concluded that adult pandas seldom climb trees. Larry Collins, in charge of the recently acquired Washington, D.C. pandas, has reported (personal communication) that as the pandas grew heavier they showed less and less inclination to climb. Morris and most observers of zoo pandas have commented that they were notoriously awkward climbers. Of five or six pandas trailed in snow by dogs, not one even attempted to climb a tree. We did find two leaning spruce trees habitually climbed by pandas. They leaned at about a forty degree angle.

What had started out as a road turned into little more than a trail, and before noon Yan led us a few hundred feet below to a crude woodcutter's lean-to constructed of bamboos and logs with a spruce bark covering. A few old wooden bowls and some baskets littered the interior while outside a prayer tablet and an excuse for an altar was sheltered by a few pieces of birch bark. Soon after climbing back to the trail once again we came on a beautiful open grass slope overlooking a wide stretch of bamboos below and spruce trees across the valley. It was the best spot I had yet seen for successful still hunting of pandas, as there might have been a very good chance of spotting one feeding along the edge of the bamboo jungle. Immediately I thought of the possibility of spending the night in the woodcutter's lean-to and coming out to watch the slope on the first hour of daylight and just before dark when animals would be feeding.

We descended through the grass to the bamboos below in search of signs. We found tracks and sign of wild boar, panda, serow and musk deer.

The direct descent through the bamboos proved much easier than the rough going we experienced the day before. The bamboos were straighter and their density broken by stretches of open bushy meadows, thus making the chance of seeing a panda greater than in a completely forested section. We observed panda signs made certainly within the past week.

*Chinese hunters in bamboo shelter. A giant panda walked by
within fifty feet of the structure.*

We had one exciting moment during our descent when Wong's dog, the only one we had brought, started to bark furiously in the bamboos just below us. We hurried down and came into an opening just above the patch where the dog was barking and Yan whispered *"Bei shung,"* but in another moment the barking ceased and the dog came out of the bamboos and we could see it had been another false alarm. We descended without further interruption to the river bottom, where we paused before returning to camp.

Sitting on a bar I could play my glasses on many spruce trees protruding above the bamboos on the slopes above us. Suddenly they fell on a small but conspicuous white object near a spruce top and just below the summit of a ridge. I watched it for almost twenty minutes although it did not change its position. I felt quite sure I could distinguish a slight movement. It is deceiving to believe one sees an object moving after watching it for a long stretch at a time; therefore I called Dean, wishing him to watch it for a moment. Its location was somewhat difficult to indicate, but with both our glasses directed on a certain tree on the sky line I began to describe to Dean in detail how to shift his focus below this tree to the object in the corner of the field of my glasses. As I was about to show Dean the precise location I was completely startled to see it suddenly disappear.

I shall never know, but this could have been my first glimpse of a giant panda. The light on the ridge had not changed; there was little wind, and I had been gazing at it for so long I knew exactly where it had been.

Therefore its sudden disappearance, a movement just catching my eye for a fraction of a second, convinced me it had been an animal, but distance was too great, the visible part too small, to be sure what it was.

Dean went on to camp while I stayed another hour to study the slopes, but no further motion was distinguished and I had to start back unsatisfied. To have set out for the particular tree I had seen the animal in would have been an impossible undertaking at that hour, and even if I had had the entire day it would have been difficult to penetrate the separating ravines and steep slopes and dense bamboos in the hope of finding the tree. Possibly if we ever spotted a panda in a tree in a conspicuous position the animal itself would be mark enough to enable a closer approach.

I reached camp just before dark and found that one of the natives had brought in a live bamboo "rat." It is a misnomer as these gray animals look like a gigantic mole with a stub tail and about the size of a muskrat.

Our traps had already captured scores of small mammals. There has been speculation in the books by Morris and Perry that at times pandas eat small mammals. This possibility cannot be ruled out, but I found the forest floor covered with small mammal tracks in the panda country and never found fur in hundreds of droppings or saw any indication the animals had dug down into the snow or turned over logs or rocks as is the custom of the bear, hunting mammals or invertebrate items of food.

On October 28 under an overcast sky Yan and I set out for the ridge I had climbed my first day of hunting to set some traps for panda. I expected to put out two chain traps I had and I wanted Yan to set his own spear traps.

When we had climbed about a thousand feet above the river bottom I was surprised to find a new spear trap Yan had set out the day before without my knowledge. Just above the trap there were panda droppings made since Dean and I had come down three days before. This was very encouraging and heartened me to realize that my two trips on this ridge on successive days had not apparently frightened the panda of the region away. I did not see why an animal so strongly built with such an easy struggle to survive should be anything but rather dull and slow in his senses and actions. Later experience did not entirely bear this assumption out.

We toiled up the ridge to the site of the last spear trap Yan had formerly used but now in a state of disrepair. I did not see a single fresh sign of panda among the spruces. I climbed on up the ridge to the dens I had discovered in the ledges above the trail on October 24 but saw no recent evidence the panda had been climbing any of the trees, using the dens, or traveling on the ridge. All the fresh signs I had observed had been below in the thick bamboo jungle.

We descended well into the bamboos till we came to a small growth of hardwood, where I indicated to Yan I wished to rig up a chain trap as a head snare. This required almost two hours of work and experiment. The principle was simple. I chopped down a good sized tree and cut off the top some thirty feet from the butt; the tree was extended at right angles to the trail and about six feet from the small end. I fastened a rope and tied the log to a standing tree about six feet above the ground to act as a lever. It took the strength of both of us to pull the small end down; the heavier end of the log providing the weight to tighten the snare around the animal and lift it off the ground. The greatest difficulty was in making a good trip. I lacked the essential of two large nails but finally made a rig whereby the animal would pull a knot loose and thus set off the spring pole.

While we were busy setting the trap a flock of great tits gathered around us. Their bright yellow crowns were colorful.

We reached the river bottom at 3:30 P.M. and went to camp. I was greeted by the bad news that the hunter Ho had fallen while hunting birds and driven a bamboo splinter into his lip and cheek, making a very nasty wound. Anne fixed it as well as possible, and if he did not get better in a few days we planned to send him into Chengtu, where he would receive proper medical attention.

I set out with Yan to set more spear traps on the north side of the mountain above camp. Our route took us directly up the hill through the farm-lands to a brush-covered slope above. Wild boar rootings were abundant on all the open fields to the top of the immediate ridge.

Yan did not follow the trail straight up the mountain but climbed eight hundred feet above the farmhouse and swung around the north slope. A little over an hour's steady traveling brought us to a large larch tree growing out of a bamboo thicket and somewhat isolated. Yan indicated that it was on this tree that he and Schäfer had spotted a young panda in 1931. Schäfer shot it from a point some two hundred yards above; this was the second of the only two giant pandas ever shot by a Westerner up to that time.

A short distance beyond this we entered a bamboo thicket, and Yan indicated he wished to set a trap on the trail just inside the bamboo. I had seen no fresh signs, but it was an excellent looking spot for a set, so we started to cut the necessary poles and the shaft for the spear. Yan carried the commonest tool used in the region. It was a heavy machete with a blade about eight inches long, two inches wide with a short wooden handle and the tip hooked around. I used an axe I had but found this very cumbersome to handle, and only the sharpest axe blade will cut bamboos. I was much impressed by Yan's skill with his knife, and in using it myself was surprised how much work could effectively be done. One could cut a tree four inches through in a few moments. In such brush it was used both as an axe and a knife.

I was growing very fond of Yan; he knew the mountains, where the best routes were, where the different game ought to be found and above all he took a great interest in setting the traps and showed good initiative in hunting as well as in suggesting new ground to cover.

I helped as much as possible in building the trap. Yan bound all his poles with green bamboo strips which he stripped from a round stalk. With his knife he cut the top of the stalk so it was split four ways and once started he made a cross out of two short sticks, placed these in the four cuts, and neatly split them into four equal lengths. The latter were tough and had enough elasticity to make an excellent substitute for rope or string.

It required an hour to construct and set the first trap, and we soon started along the slope; scarcely a half a mile beyond the trap we found panda droppings which Yan said were five days old. A little beyond we entered another dense bamboo thicket and could see

Hunter Yan using a Ch'iang bamboo knife

plainly where a panda or pandas had been crossing the trail from the gulley above. Yan said the tracks were only two days old. We set another trap.

At 11:00 A.M. we were on our way once more. The trail we were following was indistinct in many places but Yan was skilful in picking it up once we had temporarily lost it.

The north slope of this mountain, like all those in this region, was covered with spruces or silver firs near the top, but the lower slopes of bamboos were broken up by numerous fields and high thick grass and alders. I saw a great many boar and serow tracks in the fields.

We crossed a broad open field and climbed to the upper corner near a clump of dead bamboos on the top of the ridge. While Yan made a small fire for lunch I climbed a tree on the ridge and carefully scanned the next ridge and intervening ravines but saw no wildlife.

Our lunch site afforded a splendid view of the slopes across the Chengo Valley, and I surveyed them at length with my binoculars and saw nothing. Yan said there were *bei shung* in the bamboo forest on that side; apparently they are found in any of these valleys where there is sufficient bamboo.

After lunch we climbed high up through the field and intermittent strips of bamboo forest almost to the ridge top and returned.

I set out alone on October 30, the clearest day we had yet experienced. I started up the valley, moving quietly and cautiously, looking for muntjac and musk deer or serow on the river bottom. I found very fresh tracks of serow, but did not see the animal.

I paused whenever I reached an opening in the trail commanding a view of the bamboo slopes leading up to the spruce ridges above. Not only did I search the trees but also carefully watched the bamboo slopes, hoping to see a panda feeding. Signs had suggested pandas pulled many tall bamboo stalks down to strip the leaves and bite off parts of the stalk. A panda feeding in this fashion on steep bamboo slopes might not be too difficult to spot from a distance by the movements of the bamboos.

It was truly delightful to be traveling entirely alone in such a beautiful valley. The snow-covered mountains to the south stood out in great clarity whenever an opening in the trees gave me a glimpse. In a sense I missed the companionship of Yan, but alone I felt I was more deeply appreciative of a wilderness land.

Not an animal of any kind was seen on the river bottom. Half a mile beyond the point where Dean and I had descended with Yan and Wong on October 26, the trail swung away from the stream, climbing high up on the south side of the southeast tributary. It was an excellent trail and I was interested to see where it led. I ascended through the usual belt of dense bamboo forest. Very old droppings and two old sets of spear traps were the only evidence that pandas occasionally frequented this slope.

About an hour and a half of climbing brought me to an opening above the bamboos. I was fifteen hundred feet above the forks of the stream and from my position commanded a fine view of the spruce-covered slope across from me, the mountain peaks at the head of the valley, and a clear though distant sight of the large field and bamboo slope we had investigated October 26.

I surveyed the steep slope immediately opposite and south of me. Its contour resembled the backbone and ribs of some razor-backed animal: a high narrow ridge and several steep parallel spurs running down to the gorge below me. What was most remarkable was the density of coniferous trees. I wondered at the fact that the slope I was on was so overgrown with bamboo for the first fifteen hundred feet and the one opposite had nothing but evergreens. I concluded from further observations on more distant slopes that bamboos grew higher on the south side. This may be the explanation of why Schäfer reported to me he found pandas mostly on the south side of the mountains. This forest of spruces and silver firs reminded me more than anything else of the steep slopes of large firs I had seen and worked among in the state of Washington.

The snow-blanketed slopes above timber were truly beautiful in the bright sunlight. Occasional clouds drifted across the sides, clinging like so many huge white banners to the loftiest peak. It was apparent that there was at least a foot of snow as only the crags and steeper ledges could be seen. I was close enough to these mountains to have been able to spot a sheep or takin had they been moving.

After lunch I climbed several hundred feet higher on the trail but saw I was entering a steep rhododendron ravine so turned back towards camp.

I observed several laughing thrushes and streak-billed babblers on the way down. Bird life appeared abundant for this time of year.

I hunted back to camp, always searching the slopes in view, but when I arrived a little after dark no game had been seen. It was a little discouraging to hunt for six days without seeing so much as a single mammal, except one badger, but I was not disheartened because I realized that the mammals in this type of country seek the cover of the dense brush during the day and only persistent searching combined with some luck would bring its reward.

On the trail up through the bamboos I had found feline-like droppings composed of hair and bone. I brought some back and was still more interested to have the men tell me these were the droppings of *paotzu* (a leopard), and the hair that of a takin.

Before I left we had a few minutes conversation with Yan on more habits of the panda. Little by little we were eliciting more information from this man, who may know more about the life history and habits of the giant panda than any other man alive. Through the interpretation of our cook, Jim, we learned that the *bei shung* breeds in March and the period of gestation is nine months, the young being born in January. This is probably not accurate since the Chinese have successfully bred pandas in captivity since then and have determined the gestation period to be 120 to 148 days. Possibly the interpretation from Yan was a confusion on his part. Apparently, according to the zoo people, female pandas have two heat periods, one in the fall and another in the spring. If a young panda was conceived in early fall it might well be born in January.

Yan and I walked up the Chengo Valley to the junction with the Mamogo tributary. This was wild country above the last settlement at Chengwei. We crossed the Mamogo and entered a large open woodcutter's shack where a fire was burning. A fourth person was there and I recognized him as one of Yan's friends I had seen in Chengwei.

What was my astonishment to see an enormous bull takin skull and horns and a fresh skin reposing near the fire, five blood pheasants, a tragopan pheasant and a musk deer in a basket. I learned the takin had been killed by one of the spear traps set up in another valley. Nothing could more effectively demonstrate the deadliness of this contrivance. The other specimens spoke well for the effectiveness of the native's animal traps. I urged the men to hurry back to Chengwei with the skin which we eventually purchased.

The first day of November dawned with the clouds low on the ridge, and a light fresh snow fall on the slopes five hundred feet above the farmhouse. I went alone to inspect the traps set on the east slope. It did not take me long to reach the snow belt and a little above the edge of it I came to my undisturbed snare trap.

Soon after I reached the shelter of the spruces on the lower end of the ridge I observed a striped squirrel. I was much interested to watch him darting along the trunk of a rhododendron tree. With the exception of two squirrels I had collected the previous evening and early that morning on a tree just outside the farmhouse these and a badger were the only wild mammals I had seen since coming to Chengwei.

After toiling up through the wet rain-soaked slopes it became very chilly when I reached a belt of snow.

I had to keep moving to remain warm. I saw no fresh tracks or sign of any kind on the ridge and found my second trap untouched.

I descended as rapidly as possible to the site of the spear trap and started down through the thick bamboos along the ridge, above a small stream flowing down into the tributary below. This stream

Tent pitched on the roof of a farmhouse in Chengwei. The slopes across the valley contained much panda sign.

dropped over from a high cliff, roaring loudly as it rushed down to the valley bottom. The noise I made going through the brush was therefore largely nullified by the sound of falling water.

As I was working along the bamboo-covered cliffs I received the greatest start I had had in a long time. No wind was blowing, and all of a sudden I saw some tall bamboos thrashing back and forth seventy-five yards below me. I became quite excited as I felt it must be a *bei shung* but the intervening bamboos were too thick to be positive. I approached closer and came into full view of the stalks. My heart sunk as I saw immediately that the motion was caused by clouds of spray thrown from the waterfall above.

I saw nothing else on my descent to the valley bottom and back to camp.

In a further discussion with Yan on panda habits he informed us that a pregnant panda seeks any inaccessible den in the cliff to give birth to her offspring. I gathered he was referring to such old dens as we had observed in the steep ledges overgrown with spruces and surrounded by bamboo.

Ho, who had left for Tsapei the day before, returned that night with the interesting news that one of the Tsapei men had spotted a panda in a tree, but when he fired at it with his Chinese "gun" the animal went away unharmed. They trailed it unsuccessfully with dogs. This sounded like a fabulous yarn, but I had cause to believe it for two reasons. A clear day such as October 30 would have certainly been favorable for a panda to climb a tree to bask in the hot sun, and, secondly, because we had seen an old gun in the house at Tsapei. I took Ho to Tsapei a couple of days later to verify this tale.

Ho showed some reluctance to go down to Tsapei, as he tried to make me understand the panda was now far away. My few words of Chinese were insufficient to explain that I wanted to hunt there at any rate. The trail down the valley we had come up October 22 afforded practically no lookout for game as it was bordered by steep cliffs and ledges, as well as penetrating the bamboo jungle along the edge of the stream. Therefore I walked steadily for over two hours till we came to the first farmhouse at Tsapei. Ho wished to go to the third house where he had spent the night on the way up. I gathered that the man who had shot at the *bei shung* lived there. After arriving we entered the dwelling and, as I approached the fire, I was invited to sit down and offered a cup of tea. The first thing I learned was that Don had spent the night at some spot down the valley and was expected at Tsapei later in the day. The man who had encountered the *bei shung* was pointed out to me and I asked him how far up on the slope he had seen the animal. With a wave of his hand he indicated the ridge behind and volunteered to take Ho and me up there.

We started out north of the house and began climbing an open pine-dotted slope. Of course I thought we had a long ascent ahead as I saw no bamboo low on the slope. What was my surprise to have him stop at a point only four hundred yards higher than the house. He pointed to a small pine tree fifty feet below the trail and said he had shot from the point where we were standing. Needless to say I was entirely incredulous.

To convince myself of the falsehood of his assertion I approached the tree and was completely astonished to find fresh claw marks on the bark and fresh, rather small, panda droppings at the base. To my mind this proved beyond a doubt the truth of the story. The hunter said it was a small giant panda, probably half grown.

It was most interesting as this was the last place I would look for a panda. It was apparent from the composition of the droppings it had been feeding on bamboo leaves, but the nearest bamboos on this side of the valley, as I later discovered, were a mile downstream. The bamboos were low on the south side but I had some doubt that the panda had crossed the rushing stream below. What were even stranger were the immediate surroundings of the tree. The ground was very open, a few bushes only. The slope was covered by well-beaten trails with farms high above and below. I saw that the panda's only possible under-cover approach to this tree was via some steep brush-covered ravines and ledges to the east.

The huntsman who had missed this wonderful opportunity told me he had approached the animal on the same trail we had come up. The tree commanded a full view of the farm and the panda could have easily seen him crossing the field below.

I was more convinced than ever that the giant panda could not be a very alert animal or had very poor eyesight, and was not as wild as its scarcity might indicate. Furthermore, my experience earlier in the day had taught me to look everywhere for the panda and not confine my gaze to the branches and trunks of spruce trees growing up from among the bamboos at higher altitudes.

This observation also suggested that the panda on occasion is nomadic, a conclusion substantiated by the information Yan has given us on the wanderings of the *bei shung*. The sun was out so Ho and I climbed up on the pine ridge to gain a view of the tributary valley to the east. The hunter said the panda pursued by dogs had gone up this valley three days ago. I knew I had little chance of finding him but hoped I might spot him on a sunny slope. It was doubtful that he would climb another tree for some time because whatever the hunter's old matchlock was loaded with he could not have failed to have at least stung him at such a close range.

We ascended gradually two thousand feet above the valley bottom, often pausing to scan the opposite slope.

I was much impressed by the particular ridge we were on as it was entirely covered with lovely pines. It was the only slope I had yet observed in China where this species of tree grew exclusively.

I came to a farmhouse at the very top of the ridge, and from here I could see the east slope of the tributary valley. I surveyed this at some length but saw no panda.

We ate lunch and started descending the slope by a trail, cutting down diagonally across the farm-lands and up the valley. A tragopan was flushed high on the slopes, carrion crows often circled overhead and magpies were abundant. We also saw a nutcracker and nut-hatch.

About half-way down the mountain Ho entered the house of a friend and the owner came out to invite me in also. I entered and as usual found the household gathered around the fire on the ground floor of his stone house. I was much interested to see a panda and some takin skins spread on one side of the hearth. A very small man with two hunting dogs was sitting on the panda skin. Ho told me this man had shot three pandas with the aid of these dogs. I encouraged him to hunt and told him we would buy panda skins and skulls in good condition.

Ho purchased a chicken, which he carefully put under his arm and carried back to Chengwei.

We struck the Chengwei trail about a mile upstream from the pine ridge we had climbed in the morning. I stopped once on the way back to take a quick glance with my glasses at the top of the ridge across the stream and five hundred yards above. At this moment I saw the first large mammal I had seen since shooting at the goral in Tsaopo. I regret I cannot record with certainty what it was, but I believe it to have been a black bear. I saw a good size black animal turn around in the branches of a tree and put his four paws down and descend out of sight in the high brush. It looked almost catlike in its motion, and I supposed there was a possibility that it was the black color phase of the leopard, but most probably it was a Himalayan black bear. Had I seen it a few minutes earlier I probably could have determined definitely what it was. I remained fifteen minutes watching the top of the ridge, but the animal did not appear again.

I again admired the colors of these slopes which so impressed me on my first arrival. Deeper shades of red in the maples were more prevalent then two weeks before and the sight of these turning leaves was beautiful. They were falling rapidly so the ground was almost as colorful as the tree-tops themselves. It would not be many days before only the needles of the evergreens and leaves of the bamboos remained.

November 4 was the most difficult day I had spent hunting the

Tree climbed by panda

giant panda. The weather was bad, the mist lower on the ridges than it had been for several days.

I took Wong to explore high on the east side where we reached snow six inches deep. It was another fruitless day. During the day I found fresh pheasant tracks and a little beyond the first one seen I flushed a large covey of blood pheasants. These pheasants are called *sung-gi* by the Chinese. Several flushed into hardwood trees. They were truly beautiful with their red legs, high crest, and lovely green plumage. Wong was anxious for me to shoot one, but I believed with a heavy rifle I would ruin them as possible specimens. These pheasants had been followed by a wildcat, *yea-mur*. Such a pheasant would be excellent prey for the smaller cats.

After a difficult descent through the long stretch of bamboos we returned to camp.

Carter had arrived, having spent the previous night in Tsapei. He had news of some interest. Three more goral had been collected by Kao, who used his two dogs to flush them out of the cliffs. Don reported that one of his dogs seemed to be a comparatively good one and would stick to a trail over a period of time. He also told us of a giant panda that had been seen in a tree on farm-land only a half a day's journey from Tsaopo. He told of another story of a man living high on a slope across from Tsaopo who said he had cornered a panda up a tree and when the animal tried to come down he killed him with an axe. The authenticity of these tales could not be proved. They seemed to point to the theory that the giant panda *when found* is not as alert in the wild as one might suppose.

November 5 was our second completely clear day. I started out with Yan to visit two spear traps on the northeast slope of the mountain, and the one we had set in the main Chengo Valley not far below the junction of the Chengo creek and Mamogo stream.

Passing through a grove of spruces on the trail around the shoulder of the mountain, we saw several flycatchers and a striped squirrel ran across the trail in front of us.

Within an hour of leaving the camp we came to the first trap, which was not touched. Stopping a short distance beyond it, I surveyed the bamboo slopes of the mountain opposite. Mist still hung in small clouds along the ridge tops, but the sun shone on the slope I was on. Looking southeast over the crest of the shoulder, the mountain at the head of the tributary valley fairly glowed with the early morning rays of the sun. I could never tire of the sight of this range especially as we usually saw it only at dawn or dusk.

The second trap likewise had not been visited. We went a mile or so beyond to an open hill site commanding a perfect view of the slopes across the valley. Large patches of bamboo intersected by spruce ridges seemed to offer a fine habitat for the giant panda. I laid my hopes for success of spotting a *bei shung* on a tree on the mountainside. Bathed in the hot sun, I felt quite sure any panda that was on the slope would seek a tree to sun himself on.

My confidence in spotting pandas in trees eroded steadily. I shall discuss this in the last chapter. Suffice it to say I suspect young animals climb trees far more readily than adults, and the three records I have of tree climbing by pandas were all in the more open farming country.

For over two hours I studied every nook and corner I could see. Every ravine and every tree was carefully scanned but not an animal of any kind was seen.

At 11:00 A.M. we started our descent through the bamboos to the valley bottom. It was not difficult traveling as we followed hardwood, mostly birch, openings in the bamboo forest.

Fresh boar diggings and the tracks of serow and musk deer were there in abundance. Of all the large wild mammals, the wild boar seemed the most adaptable, ranging from the highest bamboos to the edges of the plain of Szechwan. When we had proceeded about two hundred feet below the upper edge of bamboo we came upon the most interesting find of the day. This was the fresh dung and tracks of a single takin. Yan said it was two days old. I could observe where the animal had browsed off high bushes. Yan believed the animal had climbed high up on the mountain and wished to go after him with dogs the next day. It was indeed interesting to know that the takin had been within three miles of camp, and it put one on the alert to watch for them in this region.

We frequently observed panda droppings, the freshest of which was probably over two weeks old. Customarily I picked up and pulled apart at least one dropping from any group that I found, searching the contents for signs of other vegetation or small mammal hair. Only bamboo was found in all the many droppings I examined in this area.

Reaching the river, we walked upstream to visit the last trap. For the first time the clouds permitted a clear view to the head of the valley, and one of the most striking peaks of the Chiung Lai Shan range was visible. With its mantle of snow it resembled a white spire in the sky. Mist began to drift away and in a few minutes I had the privilege of an absolutely clear view.

The third trap yielded nothing and we started downstream toward camp. I sent Yan ahead. I lingered down the valley, watching the slopes on both sides until dark. I saw absolutely nothing and it seemed unusual to go so long without seeing a large mammal in a region where they were obviously numerous. I watched the open creek beds and occasional openings in the hillside hoping to spot moving game but thus far I had been unsuccessful.

It was certainly exhilarating to be able to have such a day as that one, for it made traveling a great joy even if no wildlife was seen. I never tired of looking for large mammals, particularly when all the surrounding mountains were visible.

The men reported having seen a black bear on the mountainside above the farmhouse, but Dean and Anne were up there the entire afternoon and saw nothing.

Very bad weather kept us around camp for the next two days, but we set out more mammal traps and caught fifty-two small mammals in one night. Bird life around camp was abundant. Kinglets, nuthatches, laughing thrushes, titmice, magpies and many others were commonly seen.

Anne and Dean intended to leave for our next camp at Mamogo ahead of Don and me so Anne might have a possible chance at a takin before the country was disturbed. Mamogo was wilder than the Chengwei Valley and there were no houses or farming. The snow was deeper and the temperatures colder.

I could not help but feel restless after two days in camp but no poorer days for going afield had occurred since we came to Chengwei, so I doubted if any opportunity had been lost.

A native brought in a large black bear skin and skull which he wished to sell. Apparently one offer of eight dollars did not satisfy him for he took the skin down to Tsapei in quest of some more interested customer. Later he brought it back and we got it for ten dollars.

Another mammal of interest brought in was one of the fawn-colored Chinese mink. We bought this for the collection. Apparently they are not as much of a water mammal as our North American mink. Their value as a fur-bearing mammal is almost nothing.

Finally a day dawned with promise of fair weather, and I set out alone up the west side of the mountain along the trail on which Dean and I had traveled on October 26 with Yan and Wong.

Don went up the tributary valley bottom while Dean stayed in camp to finish his letters; Anne meantime worked as usual on small mammals.

I planned to take another trail branching off lower down and around the bamboos but found after some reconnoitering that two well-beaten trails leading in the direction I wished to follow terminated abruptly. I returned, therefore, to the upper trail leading up the mountain.

The sun shone full on the opposite eastern slope and I spent nearly an hour scouring it with my glasses but no animals were seen. I continued up the trail and soon after climbing above the bamboos came into four inches of wet snow just as a blanket of fog settled in.

I traveled steadily along the slopes, intending to rest for lunch at the woodcutter's lean-to. I made the descent below the fog, where hunting would be feasible.

Just as I reached the side trail leading into the lean-to I was surprised to find fresh panda droppings just below the main trail, one hundred feet above the hut. They had been made before the last light snow as they had snow on them but were certainly no more than three days old. Apparently the animal had come up through the bamboos within a few feet of the shack below. He must have passed a day or two after Dean came by on his last day's hunt.

I could just see the opposite mountain through a thin mist so ascended back to the trail and started out across the top of the large open field above the bamboos. I was suddenly surprised to find the sun shining brightly on the slope below and on the valley and mountain to the east. The high, snow-blanketed range of the Chiung Lai Shan shone brilliantly in the sunlight. Somehow I longed to be up on the highest peak with all the impenetrable bamboo and rhododendron thickets behind me—to be able to see for miles in every direction—but I knew that such a view would be unusual in this region, and were I up there I would probably wish to be below the almost everlasting fog. As I looked at the mountain crest with my glasses I cherished the hope of spotting a band of blue sheep in the snow or even takin nearer timber line. White banks of mist floated in and created a beautiful picture. The snow-crowned summits jutting above the fog reflected the sunlight above in contrast to the dark green spruce ridges powdered with snow.

I scanned every foot of the bamboos below me, hoping to at least detect a movement among them but, seeing none, continued further along the trail to the edge of the field and a little beyond the next ravine. I sat quietly a few moments and thought I could hear the grunting of a wild boar below me, but the sound was not distinct enough to warrant investigation.

I kept my eyes continually on the edge of the bamboos some two hundred yards below and, as I was approaching the other side of the field, glanced back and immediately saw a black animal moving along the edge about two hundred and fifty yards away. It did not take a second look to convince me it was a wild boar, and I hurried back along the trail to get closer for a shot.

I retraced my steps a hundred feet and looking down saw the boar heading into the bamboo. I watched him a second with my glasses and saw his hind-quarters were facing me. As it was still early in the afternoon I knew the animal was not starting his evening meal and feared that at any moment he might disappear into the bamboos. Therefore I did not attempt to approach closer but, resting my elbows on my knees, took very careful aim and fired. Instantaneously the boar dashed into the bamboos, and I knew I had missed.

I hurried down the slope and could hear more than one animal moving off into the bamboos and realized there was no chance for a second shot.

When I reached the spot where he had been I was surprised to find Dean's chain trap in almost the precise place, and it was sprung. It would have been far too much of a coincidence to have had the animal step in the trap an instant before I shot, thus causing his immediate departure, for at the time of shooting I had been puzzled for an instant to understand how the animal could move so quickly. He might have started a split second before I shot, but this was doubtful. It was too late to attempt a hunt now through the jungle itself as I had first planned, so I climbed back to the trail and started for camp. I was pleased to have finally seen game after so many days of fruitless hunting, and I felt that success was not far away.

I returned over the trail without further incident and met Dean about an hour above camp, where he had been watching the opposite slope for panda. He told me he had taken Anne out for lunch, and they had observed two black-necked pheasants near the second farmhouse. Anne had returned while Dean climbed up to a point of vantage to watch the surrounding country until dark. As it was now quite late and getting dark we descended to camp.

I was much interested to find Don had shot two martens he had found up the valley. In contrast to the North American marten these mammals are fruit eaters and Don had first spotted them feeding on berries in a tree. He also told us he had stumbled on fresh tracks of a band of four takin. Since Dean and Anne were leaving for Mamogo in two days I spent another day in camp helping with specimens.

Dean left about 10:30 A.M. to pay a last visit to the woodcutter's lean-to where I had been the day before. I was busy packing, when Anne suddenly exclaimed she saw a black bear across the tributary valley, high on the slopes. She grabbed her rifle excitedly and prepared for a shot. I could not see the bear and found later I was looking far too low on the slope. The animal was over four hundred yards away and she fired two shots. I did not spot the animal, but both she and Don pointed out exactly where he had disappeared and, taking my rifle and accompanied by Yan, I hurried down across the stream and in about twenty minutes reached the place where he had been; we found tracks leading up the mountain through the bamboo and knew it was hopeless to try and follow the bear under such cover.

We were all pleased that Anne had at least had a shot at game in this region and hoped it was not her last opportunity.

Dean arrived a little before dark, but the fog had been so dense up on the mountain that he had been unable to see anything.

I arose at 4 A.M. next morning to have an early breakfast with Anne and Dean. I helped pack up the last of their equipment, so the final load departed soon after seven.

I spent the day helping Don clean up, care for the specimens and also made arrangements for my three-day hunt to the head of this valley in search of *yea-gnu* and *bei shung.* I had planned to take only the hunter Ho but decided also to take Kung, the owner of the house where Don was staying. He knew all the country at the head of the valley and although I disliked hunting with two men, I believed it would save time in the end—especially if anything was collected. I had great hope for success if there was at least one clear day.

The men said they had spotted a small giant panda on a large tree in back of camp when we were out, but they went in search of it without success.

Late in the afternoon the two coolies who had gone up with Anne and Dean returned to report the Sages had reached their camp at 1 P.M. and, most interesting of all, had seen two takin.

Serow

Chapter Eight

Trailing giant pandas
in the snow

NOVEMBER 12 broke as bad and unpromising as any day we had had. Fog and snow were low on the mountains, and a light rain was falling. Nonetheless I decided to climb the west slope to the woodcutter's lean-to two thousand feet above the valley bottom and spend the night, hoping to observe the edge of an adjoining open field at dusk and dawn.

I took three men with me, the hunter Ho, Kung, and a coolie, Yan. The latter came to help carry bed rolls and distribute the weight so we would all have light loads for the stiff climb ahead.

We started soon after daylight. After climbing five hundred feet above the farmhouse we reached the snow line. The snow had started falling sometime during the night. Such new soft snow is good for tracking but the impenetrable fog precluded vision to such an extent it was very difficult to see an animal any distance ahead.

New snow on the slopes of the valleys, although beautiful in a clear day, is especially difficult to contend with because it adheres to bamboo leaves, its weight bending the stalks almost to the ground. Bamboo is difficult enough to penetrate when it is standing up straight. When festooned with snow it becomes a far more formidable barrier than ever.

I took very little food; I counted on shooting some blood pheasants. We heard a flock ahead of us in the bamboo and saw fresh tracks but failed to flush any birds.

The trail to the woodcutter's lean-to, although steep, was relatively easy walking. There is always great beauty in any forest clothed in a new coat of snow. Foggy as it was, I could see enough of the few spruces near the trail to fully appreciate the loveliness of the picture. Later in the day I would gladly have given up the aesthetic qualities of the snow for the impediment it posed.

Accompanied by these mountain men, all of us toiling up the trail, I was impressed that these humans were as much a part of the wilderness environment as the animals we sought.

We arrived at the woodcutter's *pungtze* at 10:00 A.M. What was my astonishment to see giant panda tracks in the snow—barely visible but clear enough to be unmistakable. The panda had come from the bamboos below and walked within a few feet of the lean-to. It was difficult to tell how old they were, and the men said they were made the day before, but I knew they could not be sure. The snow had fallen sometime during the night, and I surmised the panda had passed while the snow was falling and might not be far away. While Kung and Yan started a fire to get warm, Ho and I set off immediately on the trail of the panda as it was easy to follow.

Theodore Roosevelt, Jr. and his brother, Kermit, secured their panda by tracking him in the snow and coming upon him in the hollow base of a tree. I knew my best chance lay in seeing the animal before it was aroused, since I doubted if it would be possible to catch up with it without dogs.

We quickly realized the problems of traveling through snow-laden bamboos. We often had to crawl and soon became thoroughly soaked. The temperature was below freezing, a few flakes of snow were falling; I was thankful, at least, to be moving to keep somewhat warm.

The next five hours held an interesting story. I was exhilarated to be on the trail of such an animal for it gave me a rare opportunity to study its habits.

The tracks climbed up the ridge above the woodcutter's hut and began zigzagging through bamboos. For the first time since investigating the panda habitat in October, I observed fresh dung composed entirely of bamboo stalks without leaves. I took the time needed to measure the size of the stalks cut off by the massive jaws of the panda. Some were bitten off at ground level and some of heights above forty inches. There were indications the animal had made use of his remarkable prehensile "thumbs" on his front feet to pull some of the stalks down. Some of the droppings contained pieces a half-inch wide, indicating he had eaten the coarse ironlike stalks of the largest bamboos he had sheared off—stalks that defy a sharp axe.

For the next few hours we were amazed to find the very large quantity of droppings made by one animal in one night's feeding. They were from four to six inches long, two inches in diameter, and cylindrical in shape. We found them in groups of one to three at estimated intervals of every one hundred yards. They appeared quite undigested. In the first two hours, by a conservative estimate, I counted forty droppings. Their appearance prompted Captain H. C. Brocklehurst, an Englishman entering the panda country after we left, to mistakenly state: "The male eats stalks up to an inch or more in diameter, while the female eats only leaves and very thin stalks. Great quantities are merely chewed and not swallowed, and are all along the tracks covered with thick greasy saliva." Droppings taken from the intestines of pandas killed in the wild would fit this description.

Following his trail took us through the densest thickets and, most of the time, I was bending over or crawling on my hands and knees to get through. It was not possible to move quietly in such cover. We could barely see twenty feet most of the time but now and then the panda would cross small openings between bamboo thickets. It had chosen a steep course, and we struggled up ledges and thrashed through bamboos. The panda was ever climbing. This encouraged me tremendously, as I knew it must soon ascend above the bamboos, and I pictured myself finding it in the shelter of some stump or ledge high up on an evergreen ridge where a noiseless approach might be possible.

As we proceeded, the tracks became more and more distinct, and I felt sure the panda had passed in the early morning. Soon the tracks appeared only an hour old, and the dung was barely covered with snow. I became quite excited and prayed the animal would seek more open country. According to Ho it was a large male, and by the size of the tracks, which measured a little over ten inches in the snow, I guessed he was right.

At the end of two hours' trailing we came to a particularly rough stretch to negotiate—moss-covered slippery cliffs and bamboo so thick our range of vision was cut to ten feet. Although we were wet to the skin and cold, the fact we were on a giant panda trail kept us going. On all fours we cleared this obstacle and immediately came to a medium-sized spruce. Suddenly my heart jumped as I saw a bare spot on the uphill side. I saw at once it was the panda's bed. About thirty droppings were close to the bed. The warmth of the panda's body had melted the snow and almost dried the underlying leaves. Extremely fresh tracks left the bed and a dropping still warm convinced me we had jumped him. It was luckless that the thick bamboo prevented our seeing him.

Let me digress at this point to describe the general topography of these slopes, as it had a bearing on the next three hours. The ridge crests at the top of bamboo growth are often like hogbacks with other ridges and spurs descending to the valley floor like so many ribs. These parallel ridges running down the sides of the mountain are separated by deep rocky and bamboo-covered ravines—some, virtual gorges. If one ascends the mountain along ridge tops the route is steep but often defined by game trails. It can be likened to going with the "grain"; when one tries to cross the slope following a contour he is traveling against the grain and, at best, is trashing, floundering, falling, and often slowed to a virtual standstill.

All the pandas we followed, with or without dogs, traveled along the contours against the grain. They did not climb but often angled to the bottom of the mountain valleys.

We were probably at eleven thousand feet when we had aroused the panda, and it had started walking following the contour. Such a pursuit I have never made! We couldn't run but tried in vain to hurry in the faint hope of approaching close enough to see him. He crossed deep ravines, traveled ledges and threaded his way through the densest bamboos. We plunged on, sometimes barely moving, crawling along ledges, slipping and falling. In one ravine the trail was so steep the panda had slid twenty feet. If there was a slight opening tangles of vines and brush caught our legs causing severe falls. On one occasion I slid almost thirty-five feet. Ho fared little better. Climbing the sides of the steep ravines in the snow was like trying to climb a steep hill of soft sand. It was difficult to get traction. Being encumbered with a rifle made it no easier.

Hour after hour we chased this great beast. In my mind's eye, here was this ghostlike black-and-white mammal deep in his native habitat, moving with ease across the most rugged terrain one can imagine. With its short powerful legs, the panda steadily increased its lead.

We became very cold. Often I had to stop and knock the ice off my rifle.

Finally, the light snow falling was filling the panda tracks and we realized he was far ahead and angling down where he would soon be below snow line so we gave up the chase.

We had found additional droppings at intervals all along the pursuit trail. It was at once apparent that one animal could leave so much sign in about twelve hours to preclude any accurate estimate of populations based on this type of sign. Unlike a bear in a similar situation the panda did not run but walked the entire way. In this instance where it was known the panda had fed no longer than eight hours (from finding the track to his resting place), the amazing amount of relatively undigested bamboo excreted suggested the quantity of this food required each day to maintain this large carnivore.

We returned to the woodcutter's lean-to. Yang had returned to the valley but Kung had a large fire burning.

I spent the evening drying my clothes and warming myself after my usual meal of a roasted corn-meal cake.

To be camped in such a lean-to in the cradle of the panda mountains and to watch the firelight casting flickering beams on the oriental faces of my two companions evoked a romanticism and emotion difficult to describe. We were able to communicate by my knowledge of a few words of their language and by active gesticulations. These hardy mountain men had no blankets but slept as close to the fire as possible. For firewood they used a long log with one end in the fire. As it burned they simply pushed the log farther into the flames, finally burning it from one end to the other. As the flame

Yenshuigo Valley

burned down they edged closer, reminding me of a dog trying to get warm on a cold night by a camping fire. My weeks of close association with the ever cheerful Ho had elicited my deep affection; even after forty years I can remember him as clearly as if it was yesterday.

I spent a comfortable night with my bedroll stretched on a raised platform of poles.

I was somewhat disappointed to find that four more inches of snow had fallen during the night, for I knew this would probably obliterate the panda tracks and make further pursuit impossible. I had planned to follow the animal that day, hoping to surprise it during its day's rest. I knew this would only be feasible if the panda kept high on the mountain where there was more open country. However, under any conditions I determined to follow the trail beyond the camp across the open field and see if I could find his track coming down through the bamboos on the other side.

Three of us set out as Kung wished to show me some takin country further up the valley, where I wanted to go if I found there was no chance of trailing the panda with success.

We crossed the top of the field and descended into a ravine on the other side entering a thick bamboo forest where many large pines and spruces were growing.

I was in the lead, and not more than a mile from camp I could make out faint panda tracks in the snow along the trail. I pointed them out to Ho, who shook his head, but when in another fifty feet we came to the unmistakable tracks in deeper snow coming down to the trail from the bamboo above, the men immediately said *"Bei shung."* The tracks were very faint on the trail, and the animal had obviously hit it and started toward camp but turned off down the slope in less than a hundred feet, but there was too much new snow to find exactly where he had left the trail. His tracks could probably have been picked up again by us below, but I knew such a procedure would be useless as the entire mountainside to the river bottom was dense bamboo. What interested me was that these tracks came down the ridge from almost the exact spot at which we had left the trail the day before. The panda had made the greater part of a circle from the time we first found his tracks the previous morning. It was also obvious that at the time we gave up pursuit he had descended well down the mountain and would have been out of the snow in another thousand feet.

The evidence I had just found also made me wonder if this was not a regular range of a single animal with the large bamboo forest below the field as its center. The ridge where the woodcutter's hut was situated was a connecting link between the bamboo below and bamboo thickets high on the mountain where we had been the previous day. Tracks crossing the trail would be a natural route down on the other side of the large field.

The foot trail became very uneven and winding as we went on. It followed the side of the mountain, but the latter was cut by several deep gorges. We came into some fairly large stands of evergreens bordering the numerous creeks we crossed. These trees with the bamboos below all laden with fresh snow and the frequent cataracts spilling down through the ravines were enchanting.

After two hours of traveling we came to a second woodcutter's lean-to, showing signs of recent use. It was well padded with bamboos and in much better condition than the one we had chosen for our camp.

A hundred yards beyond this hut we climbed up through some sparsely wooded openings and came out on a fairly large field beyond. We could hear wood chopping across the valley below, and I could see two huts high in the spruces. Kung indicated that we were now in the takin pasturage, and a few old tracks in the snow seemed to bear this out. Both men showed discouragement at not finding any fresh takin tracks and wanted to turn back. The fog was really too dense to hunt further up the valley, but I went on to the further edge of the opening, and, finding no tracks, turned back. It was undoubtably a small pasturage for an occasional band of takin wandering about the head of the valley.

We retraced our steps back to camp without incident, and I dried my clothes and ate corn-meal cakes, preparing to go out to watch the field just before dark.

About a half hour before dark I took my rifle and went out to a point of vantage along the trail on the upper edge of the field and sat down to survey the edge of the bamboos below. I had been out about an hour when I heard someone coming along the trail and saw Ho coming up. Just as he reached me he pointed below and whispered "cheetzu" (musk deer). I could see the legs of the deer standing behind some brush at the south end of the field about two hundred and fifty yards off. It had obviously detected Ho moving and was looking up in our direction.

The deer kept uttering a short whistle or cluck most resembling a coarse "chuh." Every now and then it would spring with four feet from one place to another. At last it came enough in the open to make a shot possible, but a small tree intervened. I changed my position to get a shot and the animal bounded in the brush out of sight. I was struck by its alertness and obviously wild nature, and its unparalleled grace and quickness. Ho showed discouragement that it had gone, but I moved on a few hundred feet on the trail to a point commanding another view. I waited without movement for about

Trail between farmhouse and woodcutter's hut, crossed by two giant pandas seen November 17

twenty minutes but saw no sign of the deer. I returned to my former position about fifteen minutes before dark. Ho had returned to camp.

I heard the deer whistle again and spotted him below, not too far from where he had been at first. I saw a chance for a clear shot and, although it was quite far for so small an animal, it was rapidly getting dark and I could see mist coming in; furthermore, no closer approach was feasible.

I missed three shots and the fourth found its mark. I found it to be a fine specimen of the diminutive musk deer. It was so light that Ho tied the carcass on his back in the morning while I took the rucksack.

For the next two hours we struggled down through the dense bamboo. We found one interesting old rotten stump which was easily five feet in diameter. The base had been chewed out to form a nest for a panda. Many old droppings lay about, while the top of the stump was smooth and flat and had every evidence that the animal had often curled up there, probably to sun itself.

After reaching the stream I told Ho to take the deer into Chengwei while I hunted on up the valley. This stream in its upper reaches was truly lovely. Numerous gorges, cliffs lined with spruces, waterfalls coming out of the bamboo slopes above, wide-spreading rhododendron trees, and clear running water of the main stream all lent beauty to this walk. I returned to camp before dark.

A note came in from Dean and Anne saying they had not become well settled yet at Mamogo as it was cold, and the men were busy building lean-tos for their protection. Both Dean and Anne had had the unpleasant experience of being poisoned by the fumes of charcoal burned in their tent overnight. Fortunately they had not suffered any serious effects.

Winter had begun in Wassu. The next day turned out to be one of the very best we had experienced, and in no region were clear days so much appreciated. I arose early and started out to visit the two spear traps on the north side of the mountain behind the farmhouse. I planned also to visit the traps on the ridge across the valley later in the day. I sent Ho down to Tsapei to get a hunter and two dogs he knew of to have another try for the panda I had trailed two days before.

When I started, the mist was as usual low on the ridges and the last thing I anticipated was a clear day. The first and second traps were untouched and when I came out of the bamboos I was surprised to see mist blowing away and the sun beginning to shine on the slopes across the valley.

The shoulder of the northeast slope of the Chiung Lai Shan range was whiter than ever as it reflected the sunlight; its high peaks cast long shadows over its snow-covered slope. At first I could only see the end of the range, but as I started back to camp the whole range was visible, with a striking array of peaks blending into a foreground of many high and steep spruce-covered ridges leading up to timber line.

I returned to camp at lunchtime and enjoyed the novel experience of eating a meal outside in the sunlight with the majestic mountains at the head of the valley distinct in every contour. For once it was possible to enjoy the beauty of this setting to my heart's content.

After lunch I went down across the valley and began the ascent to the first spear trap on the ridge.

Since it was untouched, and no recent sign of panda was anywhere on the ridge, I climbed up to my snare trap further up the ridge and could find no sign of an animal having passed.

While high on the ridge I found a vantage point looking over the slopes across the valley; from my position I could see up the main Chengo Valley to the Mamogo tributary. Distant peaks towering above the dark evergreen ravines were washed by the setting sun, while streamers of white mist drifted up from the valley. All the mountains above the farmland were visible and I had a fine opportunity to discern the vegetation. It was apparent that the east side of the valley was not as broken up as the west side and could be described as an uninterrupted range for the panda beginning on the northeast side and extending to the last woodcutter's shack I visited three days before.

As I sat quietly, enjoying this rare view, two black-faced laughing thrushes came close by, while high above the slope two large hawks were soaring.

I remained until the sun disappeared behind the slopes and the familiar fog blew in to once more obliterate the magnificent panorama. I descended to the valley bottom and returned to camp in the dusk.

A native came in with a small female musk deer he had caught in his snare trap.

My diary of November 16 starts out with the statement "What a day of excitement and disappointment!" For almost a month I had been ceaselessly hunting the giant panda and then at last my opportunity came, and I lost it. It would be untrue not to admit the bitter disappointment but at the same time I refused to be discouraged.

Two hunters came up from Tsapei in the morning, bringing four dogs, the agreement being that the dogs were brought on trial and were only to be paid for if they proved their worth. Carter wished to go also, and I was very glad to have his company as he did not have much opportunity to get out.

Our plan was to take the dogs to the woodcutter's hut on the west side in an attempt to find fresh tracks among the bamboos in the vicinity.

Due to the late arrival of the two men from Tsapei we did not leave until 9:30A.M. In addition to the two hunters I also took Ho.

We ascended the trail up the mountain slope without delay and crossed the first large ravine on the route. As we were climbing up through the bamboo slope on the other side we entered snow that had mostly melted, with patches here and there covering the ground. Suddenly two of the dogs started whining; the men pointed to heavy imprints among the leaves crossing the trail. They said a *bei shung* had been there that morning and had gone up toward the head of the ravine.

To say the least I was skeptical, but decided an investigation was worthwhile as I intended to investigate the nearer end of the mountain the next day at any rate.

Across the deep ravine high on the bordering ridge was one of the spear traps Dean had set with Yan and Wong. I sent Ho over immediately to spring the trap so we might release the dogs. As it turned out I should have gone with him.

Don had gone up ahead, and I assumed he would not go beyond ear shot of the ravine. I found later my assumption was mistaken.

Ho appeared high on the ridge across. The two hunters took their dogs on leashes a short distance through the bamboos, and when they were sure they had them on the trail of the panda they unleashed them. I climbed up with the men high on the trail where I commanded a full view of the slope across the ravine and also would be able to hear the dogs.

Soon after the dogs were freed a single yelp was heard, and for ten minutes there was silence.

I was climbing higher up on the trail with one of the men when the second hunter, who was following us, paused a hundred feet below as if he heard something. He signaled us as we descended hurriedly. At first we heard some faint yelps and then the dogs came into full cry across the ravine and upstream from us. We ran down the trail to an open vantage point, and the next twenty minutes will stand out in my life forever.

I had been thinking of giant pandas and planning the most likely method of hunting them for seven and a half months. I had traveled more than half-way around the world to find the rarest of all animals, not seen by more than a half a dozen white men before; only two had even been shot by white men. I had hunted for almost a month on the trail of the *bei shung* and had yet to see one. The little experience I had had with dogs had been discouraging.

It was little wonder then that even with the dogs in full voice on the trail of some animal I could not believe it was a giant panda. The men began to get very excited and pointed across to a patch of bamboos four hundred yards away. I saw the bamboos moving violently, heard the dogs still two hundred yards up the ravine and saw Ho high on the ridge. The men yelled *"Bei shung!"* I called for Don and then caught my first glimpse of black and white in the bamboos. Not knowing whether I would actually ever see the animal I took two shots at the base of the moving stalks. Then the men became even more excited than before, pointing higher on the slope with the words *"Lliang gue bei shung"* (two giant panda). I could hardly believe what I was seeing when I made out another panda moving rapidly through the brush toward the ridge tops. He came out in the open well down on the ridge over four hundred yards away, exactly where Ho had been twenty minutes before. I fired twice as he disappeared over the ridge top then turned my attention to the first panda. Don had not yet shown up and I sent one of the hunters to get him.

I could see the bamboo moving in nearly the same place where the panda had first been. In the meantime Ho had descended the slope and was visible about fifty yards above the panda. As I learned later the bamboos were too thick for him to see the animal.

I got two more glimpses of the panda and fired both times with no apparent results.

The beast seemed reluctant to leave this patch of his favorite cover but the dogs were approaching rapidly. They entered the patch and then came a sight as if in a dream, such as I would travel thirteen thousand miles to witness. A tremendous giant panda came out in full view, moving leisurely but without hesitation up the slope toward the ridge top. The dogs were literally dancing around his heels. He seemed to pay no attention to them but proceeded in a determined fashion. Here I was offered my best, though distant, shot of the morning and I held the bead above and a little ahead of the panda and fired without effect, and the panda moved on, sticking as closely as possible to the brush. I was struck by his size and striking color. His hind-quarters appeared pure white but his fore-quarters and head were very yellowish. This was the rarest sight of a wild mammal a white man could see.

These pandas were obviously traveling together as the first animal was a fully adult animal and possibly a female, and the second panda appeared larger. Whether a male and female traveling together at that time of year indicated a breeding cycle is unknown.

I fired another shot as the animal was on the open slope, headed toward the ridge top. Just as he was disappearing over the top a little above where the first one had gone twenty minutes before, Don came down, in time to catch a glimpse.

When measured, this was truly long range shooting and the chances of hitting a moving animal was quite remote. How I regretted Don had not been with me during the shooting. Our chances would have been doubled.

I did not see how the dogs could lose the animal now as they were fairly running around him.

I wasted no time in running down to the stream bottom and climbing up on the ridge where the panda had last been seen. The hunters were close behind me. No sign was heard from the dogs and in a few minutes I was disgusted to have them come running up as if all was finished. The explanation was easy. It had turned out to be a clear day and it was the first time we had had two clear days in succession. Enough snow was left in the shaded ravine to make tracking easy but once the animals crossed over the ridge to the sun-dried slope above the farmland the dogs were not able to follow even a hot trail. How I wished for a couple of good American hounds.

Of course I was very disappointed, and I could view the day's experience as only another step toward success. I planned the next day to hunt the mountain behind the farmlands where the pandas disappeared. I decided also to take another day for a visit up near the woodcutter's shack. If I failed during these two days, I would have to go on to Mamogo but I certainly hoped for a few days in that valley when there was more snow on the ground.

At any rate I felt highly elated at least to have seen the pandas and to have had my chance at them.

It was hard to say how much these animals had been alarmed. From their appearance they had seemed reluctant to move at all and never traveled at more than a fast walk. The men thought they would go a long distance during the day, but I wondered.

Soon after daylight on November 17 I was on my way up the mountain with the two Tsapei hunters as well as Ho and Kao. The latter was the only one in camp that knew the location of one of Dean's spear traps. I knew this was high up on the ridge above where the panda crossed over and I intended to go up to it and work from there along the crest of the mountain, behind the farmlands, in the hope of picking up the track of one of the *bei shung*. I was familiar with the extensiveness of the bamboo growth on this range and believed that the panda must have passed over the shoulder above the farmhouse and around on the northeast slope where Yan and I had previously set two spear traps. What I was uncertain of was how high the panda had climbed, and I knew if we did not hit their track above snow line the chances of following it would be poor. My disappointment of the day before was somewhat alleviated when I arrived at the place where the panda had crossed over the ridge, for, on a careful sighting of the opposite slope, I believed my shots had been at least four hundred and fifty yards.

We climbed steadily up the ridge through the bamboos until we arrived at the trail along the top of the ridge, a good thousand feet above where the pandas were last seen. There was sufficient snow on the ground to quickly determine if any panda had crossed the top.

We found a woodcutter's lean-to along the trail and paused here for a few minutes of rest. Our location was high on the south shoulder of the mountain; we started down through open woodland along the edge of a bamboo forest running up the mountain. The hunters wished to descend directly down until they struck a track. I sincerely hoped the track would be above snow line as, if the animals had passed below it, the dogs would be useless.

A little after 9:00 A.M., about five hundred feet below the woodcutter's shack we came upon the track of a single panda made the day before. It was clearly visible in the wet snow and for the first hour the men had no trouble following it. Although the tracks were easy to follow the route chosen by a giant panda was not, as I have learned, the easiest for a man to travel.

Up one ravine and down another, through bamboo thickets and across groves of hardwood trees and heavy undergrowth.

Obviously the panda was traveling as there was no sign of the animal pausing to have a bite to eat. Two droppings consisting of bamboo leaves and stalks were found. The dogs, of course, showed no interest in the tracks as they were far too old. During our third hour of walking we came out on one of the high open shoulders of the southwest slope, where the sun had melted all the snow. The men had some difficulty in picking up the track on the other side but finally were successful. In a few more minutes we stopped in a small opening among the bamboos for lunch.

I was puzzled as to the whereabouts of the panda, for I knew from previous observations the bamboos on this slope terminated beyond the next steep ravine, and there was no extensive bamboo cover further up the northeast side of the Chengo stream. Possibly the animal had cut up to the top of the mountain and come down far upstream; a second possibility was that he had descended by the next ravine to the valley bottom and crossed to the high bamboo forest on the north side. A third possibility might have been that he circled below us near my trap and fed high back along this slope. I thought of all these but was pessimistic and inclined to agree with the men that the *bei shung* was *du de hina* (far away). Had we come upon the signs of his feeding I would have been more hopeful.

Not a hundred yards from our resting place, over the shoulder and at the bottom of the next steep ravine, we came on panda droppings that looked quite fresh. The dogs suddenly got wind of the animal and the men unleashed them. The panda had obviously stopped in this ravine, and I would estimate it had taken a little over two hours of travel from where I had fired my last shot the previous day, assuming it was one of the pandas seen the day before, a speculative conclusion. Two hours' travel for a panda would mean six for a man.

In a few seconds the dogs were in full cry heading directly down the gully bottom, and we started out. I have never made such a rapid descent through dense bamboos. With all the excitement I could not help laughing at the spectacle of the hunter Kao just ahead of me. He was fairly plunging down through the dense stalks and I was sliding down right at his heels. He slipped and his headband got caught on the broken end of a bamboo stalk. The latter ripped it off his head and I can never forget the picture of his clean-shaven head disappearing into the bamboos below with his bandana streaming out like a banner behind him.

The excitement was short lived. As soon as the panda got below the wet snow the dogs gave up chase, a chase which had lasted a mere ten minutes.

The hunting for the day was obviously ended and our chances at the panda had been reduced to zero because of the density of its cover and the lack of snow. From the experience of those two days I learned two important pointers about hunting with native dogs. When snow is scant the scenting ability of the dogs is very limited and one's chances at a panda are only good the first few minutes of chase after the animal is jumped. Also pandas chased by dogs seem to travel along a contour line and often go downhill. The best system would have been not to unleash the dogs until the men with guns, the more the better, were spread out for some distance on each side, even if in dense cover. Had this plan been followed out I do not doubt there would have been at least one giant panda in camp.

We descended to the river bottom and returned to Chengwei to find that a native from Wenchwan had brought in a fine green skin and skull of a female panda shot in that vicinity.

Golden monkey

Chapter Nine

The romantic headwaters of Chengo Stream

I set plans to go to Mamogo while Don stayed over a day at Chengwei to attend to the panda skin. We finally purchased this for the equivalent of ten dollars U.S. currency. I learned it had been shot up a tree about seven miles from Wenchwan.

I left with the last load but did not stay with the coolies. I took Ho and walked directly up the Chengo Valley, arriving at the Mamogo tributary six miles from Chengwei. I had formerly been there with the hunter Yan, but the trail up the Mamogo Valley was new and interesting. There are three main tributary streams in Chengo Creek in the western section. The Mamogo is the first tributary, flowing in from the north. Further to the west is the Dabeishuigo (valley of the clouds) and the third is the Yenshuigo, as well as the main branch of the Chengo River. All of these are several miles west of Chengwei and their headwaters are in the high towering mountains visible on a clear day. The Mamogo in its lower reaches is by far the flattest, with the bordering slopes rising less abruptly than the other branches. The hunters said it was the only one inhabited by the giant panda, but we were to find giant panda signs in the other branches as well. Some of these slopes had apparently been burned at some time, for there were many charred stumps and bare cliffs above the bamboos, particularly on the north side. Serow and goral were found there and on all the bordering cliffs of the Chengo Valley. I observed their tracks in one place on the river bar just under some cliffs.

For the first two miles the trail wound along above the narrow Mamogo stream which ran from the valley above, rapidly spilling over rounded boulders as it made its way to join Chengo Creek. Bamboos grew in profusion along the steep banks, but on the third mile the valley bottom opened out into a series of meadows divided by patches of bamboo. Spruces covered the summits of the slopes and the sides of parallel ridges rising abruptly from the meadow. Fog covered the higher ridges, and I regretted I was not able to view the great towering peaks that must rise from each side.

In an hour's travel from this fork we came on a shack with a large bin inside. This was filled with fine ashes and I found out later from old Yan that the name Mamogo is taken from a kind of Chinese medicine made from ashes of burnt meadow grass.

Wild boar rootings were to be seen in every opening, while occasional takin droppings warned me we were approaching the favored habitat of this interesting animal.

About five miles above the fork the trail followed along the rocky bank with spruces dividing the lower meadows from those I was just coming into. As I came out of a patch of bamboos I saw smoke rising ahead and in a few minutes came into sight of the camp, situated on a large flat meadow.

Three tents were pitched, and a large fire was blazing in front of one. In the foreground the men had required only a day to construct a fine three-room bamboo house giving them adequate shelter during our stay. The walk had taken me two and a half hours from Chengwei.

It is always a rare pleasure, after members of a trip have been separated, to meet and discuss our respective experiences. Dean was out exploring but Anne told me their news. No meat had been obtained, but she described the two takin they had seen in the lower valley and a boar on the slope above camp. The best news of all was the weather. The temperature was lower than at Chengwei. Some fog covered the upper stretches, but there had been no rain. The high fog permitted a greater range of vision. Much mist was converted to light snow at that time of year possibly due to the lower temperatures, which hovered around 20° F. It was truly a relief to be above the rain belt and into the snow. The altitude of the camp was eighty-six hundred feet, according to Dean's altimeter.

Dean came in during the afternoon, having climbed three thousand feet in the Dabeishuigo Valley without finding anything.

After an early breakfast the next day Dean and I set out to reconnoiter the valley above camp for signs of small mammals. Dean was also anxious to show me some of the open meadows where takin sign was abundant.

The ground was covered with a light coating of ice and a powder of snow lay on the tree limbs. It was clearer than the previous day, and I could see how abruptly the spruce ridges rose on each side of the valley, running up to timber line below the high peaks invisible above.

We made our way up the stream bed through patches of heavy underbrush with birches and maples bare of leaves. The rocks and fallen logs bordering the stream were covered with ice while here and there the spray of a small waterfall had formed icicles under the overhanging cliffs on either side. There was more aridity and snap in this winter atmosphere than I had yet experienced in this region.

We passed rock walls and ledges bordering the edge of the narrow valley. When we had proceeded a mile and a half from camp the valley turned west and opened out into two broken but extensive meadows on the east side. These were literally covered with takin tracks and dung, although there was no fresh sign. It was obviously a favorite takin pasturage. There were also tracks of wild boar, musk deer, and serow. There were deep ravines and narrow tributaries on each side. On a clear day takin could have been spotted traveling along the adjoining slope for there were many openings in the spruce forest and long ravines running three thousand feet up to the grasslands above.

After crossing the stream and examining the takin pasturage for fresh sign we returned to camp by following a trail down the opposite side of the valley.

I found some interesting runways under the sand in the various stream beds. Traps set in these yielded some of the interesting long-tailed voles.

Birds did not seem to be abundant in this valley. We observed and collected a three-toed woodpecker. I saw one flock of titmice. We observed several of the common laughing thrushes and Don saw a mandarin duck on the Chengo stream.

This was by far the most delightful and lovely camp we had had. Camped in the meadows surrounded by great mountains, and with fresh water and an abundance of wood near at hand, it reminded me of many a camp I had had in western Canada. For the first time Don and I had the pleasure of sitting in front of a large camp-fire and watching a nearly full moon dimly screened by a ceiling of fine mist rising above a neighboring spruce ridge top.

It began snowing in the late afternoon the next day and the thermometer dropped to 20° F.; it had not been higher than 28° F. all day. Don set out the remaining small mammal traps and also took a tramp up the valley to observe the takin pasturage.

We arose before daylight the next day to find six inches of snow. It had ceased falling and the day was relatively clear. I was anxious to start out in the field, but had to stay in camp in the morning to take care of specimens. We had decided to send Fung to Wenchwan to get more money via Chengtu and check on the position of the Communist troops; the political situation might make it imperative we leave abruptly to get our equipment and specimens out. In addition we were most anxious if possible to purchase some golden monkey skins and the hunter Kao was sent with Fung both to hunt the monkeys himself and to try and purchase some skins from native hunters. These skins had real commercial value and varied in price from ten to a hundred dollars depending on the length of the fur.

At 11:00 A.M. I started up the tributary valley immediately above and west of camp. It was in this valley Schäfer shot a big bull takin in 1931. As I fought my way up through the snow-laden bamboos along the creek bed I observed the tracks of one of the smallest species of wildcats found in this region. Occasionally I saw the small tracks of a mouse and once the tracks of a pheasant in the fresh snow, but I observed no other signs of wildlife all afternoon.

As I climbed up the stream bed over piles of broken rocks and through ice-covered brush the snow became deeper. I could feel a snow crust under the fresh snow of the night. When I had climbed three miles above camp to the fork of the stream the snow was a foot deep, and the steep climbing along the brush-covered banks was slow and rough. Every stone and twig was covered with ice, while the snow crystals clinging to the ice-laden limbs of the spruces and the hardwoods made a perfect picture of winter but unfortunately made traveling extremely difficult and unpleasant.

I toiled up to the shelter of a spruce tree on the southwest branch just above the forks. I could see well up some open ravines running up the side of the mountain and could see that further ascent would be useless as the fog ceiling was only five hundred feet above me. I lingered a few moments to eat some chocolate but became so cold I started back in half an hour.

When I reached another large spruce tree in a grove of bamboos a few hundred feet above the meadow I made a small fire of dry bamboos to get warm and also to thaw out the ice on my rifle.

It snowed hard for two hours in the evening and suddenly stopped. As the moon was rising in the east and the heavens cleared we were treated to one of the rarest pictures of alpine beauty we had yet had the pleasure of enjoying. Peaks down the valley and up the tributary I descended this afternoon were clearly visible, virgin white with a fresh covering of snow. Not only the peaks of the grasslands but the snow-covered spruce ridges reflected the white light of the moon and phantomlike fairly glistened against the clear sky. It was a romantic and enchanting land.

The thermometer had dropped to 17° F., the coldest we had yet experienced. Cold clear nights did not last long in western Szechwan. We had hardly time to drink in the beauty of our surroundings when clouds of mist, at first beautiful because of their reflection of the moon's rays, closed around us. This was a picture I would never forget and made me aware that the spruce ridges did not terminate just above the fog ceiling, so every clear view of the awesome peaks above was one I could never tire of appreciating.

Practical jokes and snow fights in camp had become the vogue during the past few days, and that night was no exception. Ho, Hsiang, Wong, and I were the chief participants. The Chinese could not throw a snowball so were at a disadvantage, but they delighted in these childish activities.

November 22 was my first day of looking for takin and, although not so much as a fresh track was observed, I had a most enjoyable day.

The morning broke with hardly a cloud in the sky and there was every promise of a fine day. Dean had planned to hunt on the west slope of the Mamogo and meet Anne at the forks in the afternoon. They intended to camp there and hunt takin for two days up the Yenshuigo.

I started out with Ho and proceeded up the main valley of the Mamogo stream with the intention of climbing high up in search of takin tracks.

With a fresh blanket of snow covering the ground it was certain that any tracks observed would be fresh. Working our way up through the underbrush of the stream bottom and under the overhanging bamboos along the banks I noticed many shrew and mouse tracks but, of larger animals, only the tracks of musk deer.

The sun was shining brightly and the fresh snow and ice covered forest fairly glittered. Due to the narrowness of the stream bottom and the abruptly rising spruce slopes on either side I was not able, at first, to get any view of the peaks and grasslands above.

After traveling for an hour and a half we came to a woodcutter's lean-to where the first large tributary from the west flowed in above camp. I examined with my binoculars a rugged peak almost above me.

At the woodcutter's shack the snow was eight inches deep, but walking was not difficult, and the sun added a great deal of warmth as one plunged through the thick bamboos amidst showers of snow.

From the shack we began climbing up the east slope. I wished to search for takin tracks near the ridge top, and also, if possible, gain some view of the grasslands across the valley. At first the ascent was steep but easy, as our route lay up ledges through open spruces where the underbrush was sparse. Once we had gained the crest of the ridge running up the side of the mountain I was strongly reminded of my pursuit of the panda on November 12. The going became very rough.

On our hands and knees much of the time we struggled up the ridge through thick bamboos. Finally they began to thin out after we had climbed for over two hours, and I judged we were two thousand feet above the river bottom.

Coming out on a spruce-covered ledge in a patch of sunlight we built a fire to get warm and eat a bite of lunch. From this pinnacle I was afforded a marvelous view of the mountain at the head of the western tributary. It was indeed a good-looking spot for wildlife. The stream flowed out of a tremendous basin surrounded by a knife-like rim of closely serrated peaks. Its lower reaches were overgrown

Head of Mamogo Valley

apparently exclusively by rhododendron and the snow looked very deep. Not only could I see every opening below the peaks clearly but I could also see many open ravines running from timber line to the valley bottom.

Mist kept blowing in but never stayed long enough to seriously interrupt my careful search of the grasslands and rhododendron forest. I looked essentially for tracks, and in one place believed I could plainly distinguish the footprints of a large animal along the edge of the rhododendrons at timber line, but saw no takin. I estimated that over three miles of timber line in addition to open slopes below the peaks opening to the forest were under my vigilance off and on for almost three hours, but I saw no evidence to make me believe the takin frequents the higher altitudes at that time of year. I saw no reason why they should because the snow is deep and food must be difficult to obtain.

I could make out what I believed was some sort of a cairn on the sky line along the summit of the range west of me. I was struck by the beauty of the scene, the great steepness of the spruce forest, the snow-covered rhododendrons above and the white slopes of the high peaks, one immense white blanket sprinkled with outcrops of dark crags and an occasional wind-swept summit.

We descended the slope after climbing horizontally along its upper reaches and seeing no tracks whatever. We climbed down a very open ravine where for once the snow was an assistance as it made better traction and fast traveling possible. A flock of blood pheasants were scared out before us, while here and there we saw the tracks of a musk deer.

Reaching the trail late in the afternoon well below the wood-cutter's lean-to, we started back for camp.

When we reached the large open meadows a mile above camp I sent Ho ahead and waited until almost dark in the hope of spotting takin. I saw a lone cock blood pheasant as he strutted ahead of me on the path but otherwise nothing. I reached camp at dark, cold and hungry. I had seldom enjoyed a single day of exploration more.

We woke early with the thermometer at 16° F. The day was very clear and showed no signs of clouding up. Don started for Chengwei after an early breakfast, while I stayed in camp to measure and tag the small mammals brought in.

After the mice were ready for the men to skin I set out up the valley with Ho. I started for the first large tributary above camp flowing in from the east side.

The sun had not reached the valley bottom and the relative aridity and cold were exhilarating. I tramped up the river bottom in the frosty early morning air with snow-covered ranges peaking above the spruce ridges at the head of the valley and a whole series of peaks visible south of the main Chengo stream.

At the first large meadow we turned east up the valley coming into it and were soon working our way along the creek bed through light underbrush still covered with snow. I did not encounter difficult walking all day in contrast to the day before.

Less than a mile above the valley mouth we began to climb up the north slope and found it so steep that altitude was gained rapidly. We toiled up ledges and steep ridges overgrown with fine large spruces. Where the snow did not cover the ground we saw a great deal of grass growing, and here and there observed the dung of takin and sign of musk deer. It was a most enjoyable and invigorating ascent up these ledges, although in places they were very slippery and steep so that I had to take care choosing my footholds. Bamboos and underbrush were very sparse and most of the time I could see through the spruce tops down the Mamogo Valley to the glorious vista of snow-covered ranges beyond.

About fifteen hundred feet above the river bottom we came out on an open ledge commanding a clear view below. I stopped here for lunch and took photographs. This was by far the most beautiful complete view of this alpine country I had seen since the last clear day above timber line. In fact, directly south of me I could see every detail of the contours high on the crest of the Chiung Lai Shan range. I could see the high peaks on either side of the basin where I had stalked a band of fifty sheep one evening.

Lying between the peaks and a little to the west was the Hogantu Range rising immediately above the Chengo Valley, while at a great distance a spectacular array of high peaks could be seen toward the head of the Yenshuigo branch. Still closer at hand, immediately across the Mamogo Valley, was the high range I had observed the day before.

Every ridge beginning at a stream bottom rose abruptly and eventually became a spur of one of these high mountain ranges clearly visible in the bright sunlight; I rested for an hour to enjoy a sight I knew I might never see again.

We clambered higher up the slope and were pleased to come to a series of steep open ravines full of grass and bushes; it was a very good-looking spot for takin and tracks two days old in the snow encouraged us. Since the leaves were all off the bushes with the exception of rhododendrons and bamboo I obtained a clear view of the slope at the crest of the ridge and well up the valley. Moving animals would surely have been spotted.

When we were twenty-five hundred feet above the river where we could look almost directly down on it, we began walking up the main valley along the slope and gradually began descending to the river bottom.

I saw giant panda tracks probably two or three days old in one ravine. Panda droppings were deposited at frequent intervals in the scattered bamboos, so I was on the alert for the elusive *bei shung.*

I came to one ledge, below a high cliff and well sheltered. It had been used as a resting place by pandas, takin and serow. I saw fairly fresh tracks of the latter. On this same series of ledges I saw great cracks making caves running well into the side of the mountain. I could see no evidence of these being used by any kind of mammal.

I followed ridges running down with open ravines on each side. I could move quickly and could see the slope for three hundred yards on each side.

I found a good-sized bird's nest built around three stalks of bamboo, and put it in my rucksack for the interest of the others.

Seeing no fresh tracks of any kind, we started for camp after reaching the trail at the river bottom and arrived half an hour before dark.

A bright full moon shone during the night, and dawn broke promising another clear day. Three clear days in succession is really remarkable for this region and I spent another delightful day in the mountains.

Not long after daylight next morning I set forth with Ho up the tributary flowing in from the east directly across from camp. This was a narrow valley well sheltered from the sun, with four inches of snow still lying along the creek bottom. We went scarcely half a mile above its mouth and began ascending the north slope. In choosing this side I soon found I had made a mistake as the snow had not melted and became deeper as we proceeded. However I was at least afforded a great view of the southern slopes of all the ridges up the valley.

Our route first lay up through an open ravine, but when this became so steep footing was uncertain I crossed to the top of the ridge running to the crest of the range above. It was extremely steep climbing since the ground was covered with snow and ice, making it treacherous and slippery. By holding on to rhododendron stems we pulled ourselves up over the ice-covered ledges.

We climbed steadily for three hours, until we reached the top of the main ridge. We must have been near timber line as only a few spruces grew among the thick rhododendrons. There were two feet of snow and I looked with envy on the dry slopes to the south, where the sun shone with full force.

There was sufficient crust along the ridge tops to support our

Panda country, with bamboo leaves in upper right

weight and we traveled fairly rapidly still higher till we reached the spot where the sun's rays penetrated. We rested there, enjoying the welcome warmth.

From this location I had a magnificent view of the Mamogo Valley and all its tributaries. The snow-covered ranges I had admired the previous day fairly encircled me, and I searched them carefully with my glasses. I spent most of the time watching the low open ravines on the southern slopes of the ridges up the valley. I was quite astonished at how much of the slope I could see and expected at any moment to spot a takin. During the day the animals would probably be resting in the shelter of some spruce-covered ledges but had one been feeding or traveling I would have an excellent chance of spotting him.

In descending the ridge I kept pausing to survey the opposite slopes above camp and was able to make a good study of the land contours for future investigation. The slope on the south side of the tributary flowing in from the west above camp was full of open pastures and I certainly intended to explore it in the near future. I never tired of looking at the great peaks above and somehow longed to be high on the summits with all the bamboos and rhododendrons below me.

In one place where we stopped, a flock of small titmice flew around us. Just below the point where we had hit the ridge earlier in the day we came on the large track of a lone bull takin where he had passed at least three days before. He had obviously been traveling as I could observe no signs of his feeding. Still more interesting, lower on the ridge in the bamboos were the tracks of a panda, scarcely two days old. From the signs he had been feeding up the ridge. We observed fresh droppings of bamboo stalks which had been bitten off. These animals were certainly not as scarce as one might believe.

Before plunging down the slope to the thick brush I paused for one last view of the south side of the ridge just across. Suddenly, about five hundred yards off, I picked up a serow feeding in an open ravine. It appeared almost glossy black as the sun shone on it. It passed almost immediately out of sight into the bamboos but there were open ravines on the other side and I hurried down the slope through the heavy snow in the chance of seeing it at closer range.

Just as we started our descent fog rolled up from the valley bottom for the first time in three days and hung there until nightfall. My chance at the serow was lost.

It was very steep and slippery going down and in one place I slipped and fairly shot down the slope fifty feet before catching myself on a stump. We waited half an hour for the fog to lift but it persisted, and we reached camp just before dark.

The last four days had been among the happiest of my life. Even if

I failed to secure either of the two most coveted animals of this region, the takin and panda, I felt I should never have a more enjoyable time. Of course I would have been disappointed not to succeed, but at the same time I felt the pleasure and interest I have reaped from every day afield would by itself warrant the journey half way around the world.

All the others were down at the forks, and I was to have the next three days to hunt alone in the valley.

Leaving Don to break camp I started out with Ho up the ridge immediately west of camp. The climb to the crest was steep but easy as we crossed an open brush-covered field. Once on top we started climbing west up through the bamboos along the crest. It seemed to be a fair trail so traveling was not difficult.

As soon as we reached the spruces the trail became well defined, and the ascent proved to be a most enjoyable walk. Not long after we struck the bamboos we began to see panda signs and came on old tracks in the snow. Soon after starting up through the spruces we came upon the track of a large panda, apparently not more than a day old. There were about four inches of hard snow on the ridge, and the animal's footprints were very clear. A light powder of snow had fallen in the night, and this covered the tracks, indicating they were at least twelve hours old.

I was interested to see the panda had traveled along the trail directly up the ridge. Heretofore I had only found evidence that they had crossed trails. Following this animal was quite a contrast to our previous experience at tracking the *bei shung.* It was an open heavily timbered ridge with fine spruce trees and rhododendrons but little underbrush, although there were bamboos on the south side. Here and there the panda had paused by a large spruce; from the signs he had apparently scratched the bark and dropped back on all fours, similar to behavior of the North American black bear. I believed the panda was simply traveling the ridge top, since the north side contained only rhododendrons while the south side contained bamboos. Again this would have been a very logical spot to place a trap to catch a panda alive, since it formed a bamboo edge.

We saw older panda tracks in several places which may or may not have been made by the same animal. If they were the same it would certainly have indicated that this particular animal was quite local in its habitat.

Finally we reached a point where he turned down into the bamboos on the south side. There was no panda sign on the north side of the ridge in the rhododendrons. I knew it would be hopeless to try to pursue him under this thick cover, especially when the tracks were probably a day old and there was little snow on the south side. Later in the day we came on the track of probably the same animal on the same slope, but since the snow occurred only on the most shaded areas of the ravine it was not possible to follow the track.

In places the sun shone through the heavy branches overhead and, as we proceeded on the trail, we enjoyed occasional glimpses of the mountains on each side.

I left the trail to cut across the side of the slope in an attempt to hunt on some of the open ravines I had seen from a distance the day before. I hoped later to follow this ridge trail further, as I believed it went directly up the ridge to the mountains and grasslands above.

I soon found that a slope appearing fairly open at a distance is a different problem close at hand. As I have previously observed it was always most difficult traveling in this country across the slope because the bamboos usually point downhill and it was a continuous struggle to push through them to go up and down parallel ravines.

I was much interested by the amount of panda sign, old and new, and kept careful lookout on all the trees visible on the slope in the hope of spotting a panda sunning himself.

Finally reaching the top of a fairly open ravine for lunch, I had a very close and clear view of the mountains at the head of this western tributary but saw no tracks. This seemed to definitely indicate that in the short time left at my disposal hunting takin above timber line with the additional time it would require would be little less than a waste of time.

After lunch we started back toward camp, returning lower on the slope and walking as quietly as possible in the hope of seeing game of some sort. We saw some old takin signs high on the slope. Nearer the river bottom we came upon the dung and tracks of a single takin, maybe a week old.

As usual musk deer and muntjac sign was very abundant while pheasant tracks were often seen. We saw nothing animate during our descent of the slope. Finding the going so noisy I attempted climbing trees, but these did not give me a much better view. If I had had climbing irons and could have gone up some of the large tall spruces, I am sure the chances of seeing game would have been greatly increased.

We descended to the tributary bottom about a mile above camp, reaching it at 4:00 P.M. as the fog was rolling in.

It was a lonely deserted looking camp to come to and find only one tent and two men, but somehow I enjoyed being alone for two days and only hoped I could find some of the elusive animals during the next days of searching.

The next two days fog blanketed the slopes. Although we were afield all day nothing unusual was seen except a tufted deer I collected just upstream from our camp.

We broke camp on the third day and proceeded to the Sages' camp at the forks. Reaching the camp soon after 10:00 A.M., I found Anne as usual working on small mammals. Dean was hunting up the valley, while Don had gone to Chengwei to get more salt for another fresh panda skin we had purchased.

Thanksgiving Day, November 29, broke clear and cold. Shortly after breakfast, half an hour after daylight, I spotted a goral high on a ridge of cliffs down river on the north side. He was over five hundred yards off, much too far for a reasonable shot, so I suggested to Dean we attempt a closer approach. While we prepared a stalk, the goral moved to the sky line of the ridge. Dean and I started down the valley in the hope of spotting him on the other side.

We traveled about a half a mile downstream to where we could command a view of both sides of the ridge. Dean waited there while I moved two hundred yards further downstream. In a few more minutes of searching with my glasses I picked out the goral standing in some high bushes on our side of the ridge. Precipitous cliffs surrounded him on all sides and a closer approach appeared to be a long chance. Only the head, neck, and foreshoulders of the animal could be seen. He shortly disappeared.

Half an hour of searching with our glasses from different points along the river bar failed to reveal him again so we returned to camp. On our way back we saw a solitary snipe along the river bar. He flew only a short distance and lit about fifty feet away. I stayed to watch him while Dean went back for a shotgun. I was interested in watching this bird feed. He waded along in shallow water, apparently finding his morning's meal just under the water surface.

In about fifteen minutes Dean appeared with a shotgun; the bird had just fled out of my sight behind a rock but flew up before Dean spotted him. Dean pursued him downstream and finally collected him.

The man with whom I had hunted panda at Chengwei and who owned two of the dogs used had been with us several days, apparently waiting for employment. That afternoon we decided to send him up on a cliff with his dogs in an attempt to rouse the goral and afford us long shots from the valley below. All four of us went down along the river bar with rifles. We sent Ho up also with a shotgun and rifle slug cartridges in case he should see the goral at close range. It was a great mistake that one of us did not go up with a rifle, but the cover was so thick it appeared the best chance was for a shot from below.

We waited half an hour, saw Ho appear on the sky line and later heard two shots. Twenty minutes elapsed and nothing more was seen or heard. We assumed Ho had probably shot the animal so returned to camp.

No sooner had we reached camp than I picked up Ho searching

around in the cliffs near the sky line. He disappeared from view, four more shots were fired, and we heard the dogs running. I hurried back down the river but did not see the goral or hear the dogs again.

Ho came in later and reported having seen three goral, one of which he had wounded but did not get.

A little after 4:00 P.M. we assembled for Thanksgiving dinner and a real feast it was. In the first place Dean had contrapted an appetizer using the ingredients of Bacardi rum, honey, and apricot juice. He secured ice from the large icicles hanging under one of the ridges going over the stream and an empty tobacco tin as a shaker.

Jim completely astonished us all by placing on the table delicious sausages, roast pork made from a pig we had purchased, roast Goral, hamburg steak, jellied meat, roast potatoes, string beans, raisin bread, apricot pie and to crown it all a delicious pyramid five-layer cake with thick chocolate frosting, nuts, and raisins. We finished late and finally turned in.

In the morning I took a shotgun immediately after breakfast to collect some birds early in the day. I followed the trail downstream and in crossing the tree-covered flats where the camp was situated found a flock of titmice and secured two specimens of different kinds. Titmice were probably the most abundant winter birds higher in the mountains. Besides the great tit, other species included the green-backed tit, the brown-crested tit, Blyth's long-tailed tit, and Père David's tit. I found I could call these birds within close range by squeaking with compressed lips against my hand, but after one shot the flock disappeared. Rosy finches were quite numerous and I collected one female. Among the most common birds were two species of laughing thrushes; we had so many of these I did not try to collect any.

Next morning I set off with Yan's son to explore the valley coming in just south of camp.

A light snow had fallen during the night, and I kept my eyes open for fresh tracks. I found that Yan's son knew the trail up this tributary and so let him go ahead. We saw several thrasherlike birds among the trees along the river bottom.

Fresh serow tracks crossed the creek about a mile above its mouth while a hundred yards above were the tracks of a wild dog (*yea-gou*).

A mile and a half above Chengwei Creek the trail turned up the east slope and ascended through the bamboos to a spruce ridge projecting down through the heavy forest high on the mountain slope. It was always a delight after struggling through dense bamboos to come to the top of a narrow ridge covered with spruces permitting a view on either side.

I was ahead and had not proceeded but a few hundred feet before I noticed recent panda droppings and soon could make out the faint tracks of the animal along the ridge top. It was following a generally downstream course and was probably a separate panda from others making tracks up the Mamogo valley. It was difficult to estimate the age of the tracks but they certainly had been made before the last snowfall. We followed the tracks for about a mile along the trail to where they turned down the slope into the dense bamboo, and then we returned to camp.

After supper, at about 9:00 P.M., we heard wild dogs barking up on the cliffs where we had seen the goral the day before.

The first day of December dawned without a cloud in the sky, and soon after breakfast I set off with Ho to investigate the upper Chengo and Yenshuigo tributary.

Don prepared to leave for a hunt after golden monkeys in the Chengwei tributary. He was to meet us in Chengwei on December 6.

I have seldom enjoyed a tramp more than that up the Chengo stream bottom in the early morning with the sun shining brilliantly on the beautiful mountain at the head of the valley. This mountain was very steep and rugged, with a sharp sawtooth shoulder running from the north and culminating in a spectacular peak above.

Another layer of fresh snow covered the ground. We saw tracks of mice and those of mink along the stream.

About half a mile below the western tributary known as the Dabeishuigo (valley of the clouds) the trail left the snow-covered broad river-bed and entered a flat overgrown with trees and heavy underbrush. We almost immediately found fresh tracks of a serow. Ho circled around the inner edge just below the high northern slopes while I kept on the outer edge. It was apparent from the tracks that one serow had been feeding on the flats for some time during the night.

Passing the mouth of the Dabeishuigo, we crossed the river and started up the mouth of the Yenshuigo about half a mile distant. We saw musk deer tracks on the river bottom. I was quite surprised on reaching the junction of the Yenshuigo and main Chengo streams to find a large open park-like meadow with a few large pine and spruce trees growing in it. A tumbledown woodcutter's shack was in the center of the meadow. Across the Chengo stream was a very steep spruce-covered mountain covered with a scattering of bamboos. Cliffs and ledges could be seen projecting out of the forest but enough grass seemed to be growing to offer takin pasturage. Soon after starting up the Yenshuigo I came to a woodcutter's lean-to in good condition on the west side of the stream.

This was more of a permanent shelter than any of the others I had seen and later proved to belong to the hunter Tang and was primarily a hunter's hut. It was well built and stacks of firewood stood nearby. There were several iron kettles inside and a neat assortment

Pungtze *(woodcutter's lean-to) in Chengwei*

of hooks above a stone fireplace so a kettle could be hung at various heights above the fire. A cake of salt and a wooden bowl of lard were stored in a niche in the back. He had a bamboo container of oil and a block of resinous wood; the long splinters he cut from this made excellent candles.

He had two muzzle-loading antiquated guns. They had long heavy iron barrels and short sharp wooden stocks over three inches wide. The hammer was a long piece of forked iron. When Sage visited this hut he persuaded a coolie to go with him to fire the gun.

As he described it,

> Kan put powder on the pan and took a short piece of rope which he held in the fire until the end glowed like punk. Li, the coolie, turned his head the other way and shut his eyes—a prudent measure I thought. When he pressed the trigger, the hammer brought the burning rope in contact with the powder in the firing pan. There was a loud s-s-s-s followed by a deafening explosion, and the barrel belched out a cloud of flame and black smoke, while a fistful of broken nails and stone whistled harmlessly in the bushes.

This, then, was the only type of weapon I saw at that time in Wassu. Tang claimed to have killed several takin with it. Its lethal range must have been very short.

We stopped at the lean-to a few minutes in the bright sunlight and I examined the mountain opposite with my glasses but saw nothing. Proceeding up the Yenshuigo we found fresh wild dog tracks crossing the trail but observed no tracks of a possible prey species.

The Yenshuigo was a beautiful stream spilling down past a sheer rock wall on the east side rising in a series of cliffs to a high spruce ridge above. The ledges were crowned by trees and bushes laden with ice and snow, while frozen waterfalls on the high cliffs above were festooned with long icicles glittering in the bright rays of the sun.

Only a mile above the mouth of the stream I climbed off the trail up a ravine into the bamboos on the west side but found no tracks.

On the way back I was interested to observe a flock of nuthatches and titmice very high in a large spruce tree. I saw black water dippers here and there along the stream.

I spent most of the next two days collecting birds; the Sages had gone up to the Dabeishuigo for two days. On the afternoon of December 4 the Sages, on their way back, sent the hunter Tang ahead with his two dogs and a note suggesting I take Tang up the Mamogo for a last hunt in the valley.

I took Ho with me also. On the way up the dogs started on the

trail of what the men said was a wild boar. With so little snow on
the ground I was pleased to have them stick on his track for almost a
half an hour. The boar kept high in the bamboos where there was no
chance of seeing him. Reaching our old camp in the Mamogo
meadow at 4:30 P.M. I left the men and took a final hunt up the
valley to the meadows where there was so much old takin sign.

Somehow I could not help but feel a great deal of sentiment on my
last visit to this lovely camp site.

Walking quietly up the valley the setting sun painted a sky with a
pink hue and cast an eerie light on the spruce ridges with the snow-
capped peaks in the distance. The atmosphere was sharp and clear,
adding to the zest of the walk.

I found a fresh track of a large wildcat or small leopard but otherwise saw nothing. I watched the slopes till it was too dark to see and
returned to the *pungtzu* in the meadow.

I made my supper of hot tea, bread, and cold meat and wrote my
journal beside the fire by candlelight.

The hunter Tang amazed me. He wore a pigtail, the only one I saw
except that of the house owner Yan in Chengwei. He was of extremely light build but proved to be the best hunter and mountaineer
of any mountain man we encountered. The most surprising fact was
that when he came in at night after a hard day in the mountains he
ate a light meal and smoked opium until about three or four in the
morning, when he slept an hour or two, ate a light breakfast, and
arose to climb the mountain. He carried a fifteen-pound muzzle
loading gun and most of the time led two dogs on chain leashes. He
was extremely alert each day and appeared to be full of energy. He
was also the only mountain man we saw who used flint and steel to
light his opium pipe and was pleasantly surprised when we provided
him with matches.

The next day proved to be one of the most enjoyable, exciting, and
interesting of those spent searching for pandas in Wassu. We started
up the ridge at daylight with the rays of the rising sun just touching
the peaks in the west. The temperature was 12°F.; the ground was
frozen and the dry grass and leaves were covered with a coating of
frost. The air was extremely invigorating.

We toiled up through the bamboos without resting, reaching the
spruce forest high on a ridge. The sun just penetrated the upper
branches of the high trees; patches of snow still lay on the ground
and several flocks of titmice and nuthatches were feeding in the
tree-tops overhead.

I was walking ahead, carefully watching the trail for signs of
tracks. After we had proceeded about half a mile beyond where Ho
and I struck the large panda track the previous week I noticed a fresh

impression on the crust of the old snow and could see some heavy animal had been traveling the ridge. I called the men's attention to it and they immediately said *"Bei shung."* The dogs began to whine and it was at once apparent that the animal had passed that morning.

Keeping the dogs on a leash we followed its trail for less than half a mile along the ridge, where it then turned off into the bamboos on the south slope.

Here I believed was a good opportunity to hunt with the dogs. From previous experience I knew that it would be hopeless to try and follow the dogs into the dense bamboos below, so I sent Tang down with them while I stayed with Ho on the ridge to listen and see if the dogs jumped the panda and determine the direction they would go. It might then be possible from our vantage point above to move up or down the ridge rapidly and possibly intercept the *bei shung.*

Tang disappeared below and a little later I heard a faint yelp. Ho said the dogs were on the trail of the *bei shung,* but they went out of hearing immediately. By whistling we kept in touch with Tang, who sounded as if he was working down the slope and up the valley. We proved to be mistaken but were not aware of it at the time.

We climbed up the ridge into the rhododendrons and we came upon the tracks of three or four takin; the animals had been on the ridge two or three days before. Their tracks meandered about, leaving the ridge to go down into the bamboos on the south side but returning again to the ridge top.

We had lost contact with Tang so left the ridge, cutting across the south face of the mountain on the upper edge of the bamboo. Almost immediately we came upon the very fresh tracks of a single large takin. This was indeed exciting but my hopes of following him faded for the snow occurred only in patches, and we lost the track in the maze of older tracks in the thick jungle. It was impossible to move quietly on the crusty snow. I climbed a tree overlooking the next ravine up the valley but saw nothing.

We gave up the pursuit and since I had to be in Chengwei in the evening a further hunt up the valley would have taken too much time so we returned to the ridge. I certainly was reluctant to leave the freshest sign of takin I had yet found in this country.

Returning down the trail we heard Tang whistling well down the slope and four hours after we had started on the trail of the panda the dogs met us on the ridge. It was obvious the hunt was over, and we started back for camp.

It was with a very deep feeling and sorrow that I paused on the crest of the open ridge above the Mamogo meadow. For the last time

I cast my glasses on these slopes at the head of the Mamogo Valley in the hope of at last spotting a takin, but saw nothing. With deep sentiment I looked down at the lone tent in the meadow where once three tents had been pitched and everybody skinning and working.

How I longed for another week in this valley for I felt I had but skimmed the surface of exploring for wildlife. The aura of this great uninhabited wilderness was overpowering.

Tang came in a few minutes later to announce he had glimpsed the *bei shung* at a long distance running ahead of the dogs. What was my great amazement to find the animal had come down the valley and crossed the main Mamogo stream seventy-five yards below and within full sight of the tent. His tracks and those of the dogs were there to prove it. From what Tang said and from the size of the tracks I recognized it as a small animal. The tracks were barely six inches long. Without question this was a different panda from the one I had followed on the ridge a week ago. The dogs may have been on his tracks for more than an hour. Had I stayed in camp I believe I could easily have intercepted him ahead of the dogs. Following the tracks we found the dogs had left the animal near the crest of the ridge on the other side of the valley. I had hoped in vain they might have treed this young panda.

It seemed as if I was leaving this valley just as the wildlife was coming in, and how I regretted turning homeward in the afternoon. With the exception of a few days panda hunting at Chengwei our best days afield in Wassu were over.

We walked rapidly down the Mamogo and in a little over an hour reached the site of our camp at the fork. Only a smouldering fire remained, as Anne and Dean had left in the morning.

A little after 5:00 P.M. I reached our old panda headquarters in Chengwei. Anne and Dean had seen not only a fresh panda and takin track up the Dabeishuigo but also golden monkey sign, the first we had seen on the trip. They also heard a pack of wild dogs running high on the slope. When the barking ceased they found a freshly killed female serow. It was only disemboweled and the eyes eaten out so was a satisfactory specimen. They also found fresh leopard tracks crossing the Chengo Valley.

In our old quarters once again I still hoped for success on the panda during the next four days. This had proved the best small mammal spot we struck on the trip and even with all previous trappings our catch the night before yielded thirty-nine mammals.

Dean and Don went with Tang up the ridge where I had shot at the *bei shung* two weeks before and reported no fresh signs on their return.

Late in the evening a hunter brought in a large takin skin and skull, and the usual protracted bargaining took place, with the final compromise on price awaiting decision in the morning. On December 7 Dean, Don and I set off up the valley with Wong, Tang, and his dogs to the place where Don had seen a *bei shung* track three miles up the Chengwei tributary.

The day was cloudy but the fog blew clear later in the morning.

We tramped rapidly up the river bottom and within an hour and a half of Chengwei found *bei shung* tracks on the east side of the river in light snow on the river bottom. Don said they had been made since he had come down two days before. Older tracks were also perceptible, seeming to indicate that a panda had been feeding in the locality for the last two or three days.

Tang started off on the trail immediately, and I proposed accompanying him, but Dean suggested we wait and see if he found the tracks fresh enough to follow. As a matter of fact the slope above was very dense with bamboos and there seemed to be a fair chance of a panda attempting to cross the main valley if jumped; furthermore, if we scattered along the river bottom three of us could gain a fine view of the slope and probably could hear the dogs if they started on the hot trail of the *bei shung.*

As Tang did not return at once Dean sent Wong on his trail with a shotgun, while three of us spread out at different points along the river bottom. I went upstream where the river bent to the west and reached a vantage point for viewing the entire slope where Tang had disappeared. There were several open ravines running well up the mountain side, and if a panda started in my direction he should have been easily visible.

I waited for over an hour but heard nor saw no sign of the dogs or man. I became very cold and walked a short distance upstream but hearing nothing returned to where Dean was waiting across the river and downstream. We were both so cold we built a small fire and ate a light lunch. About 12:30 P.M. I crossed the river and started up the trail of the man and dog. Within a few minutes I met Wong descending the slope; he seemed entirely discouraged and reported that the *bei shung* track was older than we had at first thought.

While resting a few moments by the fire a striped squirrel ran out on a log nearby and quickly disappeared into the bamboos. A little later one of the small common brown shrews skipped out onto the snow about twenty feet from me and I dashed forward to catch him hiding under a bamboo stalk.

A little later we started down river for camp but I left Dean and Wong and climbed up the ridge across the river to visit the first spear trap we had set as well as my chain snare trap. Clambering up through the bamboos I saw a flock of titmice including the lovely species with a bright yellow crest. I saw the tracks of serow and

musk deer in the light snow under the bamboos but no sign of a
giant panda. I saw nothing around the spear trap that was set over a
month previously. There was a cat track going up the ridge, and he
had stepped through the head snare I had set for *bei shung.* Tang
returned later to report he had seen a takin and his dogs had also
chased a panda which he was unable to see. I returned to the farmhouse in Chengwei without further event.

Don was due to leave the next day for Tsaopo to get the specimens
there and he arranged to meet us the night of December 11 in Saochow on the Min River. Dean and Anne planned to leave within two
days to spend one night at the woodcutter's shack where I had shot
the musk deer and seen a serow. The next day, December 8, would
be our final day of searching for panda in China. I planned to go with
Dean on the mountain where Tang had been the day before.

Precipitous slopes of panda country

Chapter Ten

Close quarters with a giant panda

DECEMBER 8 had a rather inauspicious beginning. We were anxious on our last day to get off to an early start but several things interfered. In the first place there was some confusion over Don's departure as many odds and ends had to be packed and final arrangements made for our meeting in Saochow on the Min River.

Another delay was caused by the sudden departure the night before of Tang for Tsapei on the excuse that he wanted to get another dog, the real excuse being undoubtedly that he wanted to buy more opium. He did not arrive back until late in the morning, bringing a second hunter with a single red dog. A third hunter owning a single male dog also wished to accompany us. His dog was truly savage, a heavy thickset very dark-colored animal. Tang's small bitch had by far the best nose of any dog I had seen in this region. She was very affectionate and likable in great contrast to most of the native dogs. Tang's male dog had returned to Tsapei two days previously and had not been seen since. He had taken the large savage dog the previous day. This was the only dog I had seen that appeared courageous enough to actually worry a *bei shung* enough to possibly put him up a tree.

With three hunters and their dogs in addition to Wong we made quite a procession up the valley. Since Tang had been up on the mountain the day before we let him take the lead with his dog.

We tramped up the valley bottom to where we had seen the panda tracks the day before and started struggling up an open steep ravine of the mountain. Before reaching thick bamboos it was beautiful climbing up through these open woods with the sun shining through the tree branches reflected by about four inches of snow underfoot. We saw takin tracks about three days old as well as serow and musk deer tracks.

We ascended without stopping for well over an hour until we came to a crest of the ridge just north of an open series of ice-covered ledges. At the edge of this opening we beheld the most magnificent view of the mountain ranges at the head of the valley. We rested here for almost an hour, scanning every open ravine in view with our glasses as well as searching the distant grasslands for sign of life,

Sage and hunters halt an hour before our encounter with a panda in Chengwei Valley. Such small openings in the jungle are not unusual.

but saw nothing. It was a beautiful panorama spread out before us with the high peaks in a semicircle at the head of the valley. The last week of bright sunlight on the slope had burned large green patches on the southern exposure, and we both remarked how delightful it would be to be wandering about the crags and summits at this time of year, in such clear, cold, and invigorating weather.

While resting, Tang took me a few hundred feet below to the edge of a neck of bamboos running up to the open ledges, and showed me fairly fresh tracks of the *bei shung* he had followed the day before. He indicated the animal had circled below, headed high on the slope down the valley in a northerly direction. I was surprised to see more and fresher sign of takin than I had observed anywhere. Tang pointed out where he had observed a single *yea gnu* (takin) the day before. As another young bull takin had been purchased the previous day, we were not particularly anxious to hunt the takin on our last day when there seemed to be chance for a panda, so we told Tang to search for panda and nothing else.

We came on a panda track on the ridge which Tang seemed to believe was only a day old but Dean and I both thought it was older. As we proceeded we became convinced of it.

For an hour and a half we fought the usual difficulties of horizontal travel in the bamboo jungle on the steep slope. However there were enough open ravines and spruce-covered ledges to afford some glimpses of the country below us and this somewhat added to the interest of the search.

Although I thought there was little chance of actually catching up with the animal we were on the trail of, I wished particularly to spend my last hours of hunting on the slope where I knew panda had recently been, and there was always a chance of hitting a very fresh trail; the possibility of a shot was remote, but at the same time was our last chance. We passed several large spruce trees where the panda had paused to urinate. All the dung was solidly frozen and appeared to have been made within the past two or three days.

Coming to the southern exposure of an open ravine we paused to rest. It was an interesting coincidence, in view of what happened half an hour later, that as Dean and I sat there we discussed in some detail the circumstances of the hunting of the two previous pandas shot by white men—the first, when the Roosevelt brothers had trailed and shot an old male in southwestern Szechwan in a fresh snow of early April and the second, when Ernst Schäfer shot a small immature animal out of a tree on the northeast slope of the mountain an hour's travel above the farmhouses in Chengwei.

Taking up the trail again we struggled on. We saw a flock of tufted titmice in the branches of trees overhead. Takin tracks were occasionally seen in the exact locality where the panda had traveled.

We experienced some difficulty in picking up the track after it crossed the southern exposures of the slope, where the sun had melted the snow, and I noticed the difference in the size of a track, indicating that at different times we were following two animals traveling in the same direction.

I was sure I was right in this assumption when the larger track followed an open ravine some distance down the slope and headed in the dense bamboos, while a hundred feet below was the smaller track about the same age crossing the bottom of the open ravine.

We descended to the latter track, and, since it was almost 2:30 P.M., and we were far above the river bottom, I suggested unleashing the dogs at least on the chance they might be able to move a *bei shung*. The little bitch started right off on the smaller panda track as if there was some scent in it or it may have been possible that the dog got wind of a panda ahead as the bitch had been testing the wind and whining. She was quickly followed by the other two dogs.

The hunters ahead climbed rapidly after the dogs, although there was no barking and apparently no definite evidence of any animal ahead. While Tang and the other hunters were ahead following the dogs I was behind them with Dean, Wong and the third hunter behind me.

As we passed above the ravine around a series of ledges we saw a pile of *bei shung* droppings at an old den or resting place. The hunters' trail led across the next deep narrow bamboo-filled ravine and up through dense bamboos to the crest of a steep ridge running up the mountain. The men had started up the ridge and I followed for a short distance when Dean called from below asking if I saw anything. Strangely enough he also said it seemed a fruitless procedure, and I was inclined to agree, although I wished to put in every last minute I had on the slim chance, a chance diminishing every day and now seeming entirely out of reach. Hardly had we finished talking when the sharp "yip, yip, yip" of the little bitch was heard a little below and beyond us in the ravine. I called to Dean asking if he had heard it. He said he could just hear it but felt it was far down the slope.

Then ensued as exciting a ten minutes as I have ever experienced in my life. Two hunters were above me on the ridge, with Dean and Wong about one hundred feet below on the crest of the ridge. The dogs now came into full cry below, with the steady high voice of the bitch predominating and the intermittent lower barks of the two male dogs.

Suddenly they seemed to be getting a little fainter. Wong motioned me to move up the ridge as the animal must have been heading around and above. I started up but had hardly gone ten feet when the barking grew suddenly louder; I heard bamboos cracking

below and then a loud sonorous growl. One of the men said
"Paotzu" (leopard) and for the moment I believed them as the sound reminded me more of a large cat than anything else.

Then I heard a shot from Dean which he thought had missed. Then a second later I saw a large animal moving below in the bamboos directly toward Dean. As if in a dream I recognized it immediately as the coveted panda. It was not fifty yards below me and I fired as the panda came into full sight, still walking toward Dean, broadside below moving toward the ridge top. I knew he must have been very close to Dean. As I leveled my rifle the thought instantly flashed through my mind that I must not delay shooting as I might hit Dean if the panda crossed between us. I was sure my second bullet hit him. The animal looked to me a very dirty color below in the bamboos and not at all conspicuous.

As good fortune would have it my last shot and Dean's fourth shot were fired simultaneously, neither of us realizing the other had shot. And the animal rolled over, slipping down the steep snow-covered slope, stopping at a clump of bamboos fifty feet below, obviously killed. A photograph of this dead animal has been referred to by another author as "a sight to thrill a sportsman or chill a conservationist's heart." This is a point of view which might be disputed by saying that many of the numerous live pandas captured have died in transit or succumbed after a few months in zoos.

After weeks of climbing and hunting the panda I would be dishonest not to say our elation was unbounded at this moment. Such a fortunate coincidence of circumstances seemed impossible. It all happened so quickly we could not realize what our good fortune amounted to. For once we had been on the right ridge at the right time when the dogs had jumped a panda. It was truly impossible to believe a giant panda lay dead on the snow below us. We descended rapidly to examine the animal and found a fine old mature female. I was not familiar with the appearance of the mammary glands of a nursing female panda but, by the appearance, she had either recently weaned a young one or may have started nursing, although I could detect no milk. During the forty years since that event I often wake up at night and ask myself why I did not have the presence of mind to back track this old female and discover where she had been when the dogs started her.

With the help of four men, skinning her was completed in only an hour, and it was after 3:30 P.M. when we started for the river bottom. The panda had bitten the large male dog in the forefoot; apparently he had been biting at her flanks. While skinning her I approached too near this dog and he bit my foot, making a hole in one of my shoes.

The descent to the river bottom was steep and difficult. During the day we had worked well up the mountain and going down was very slippery. The usual dense bamboos were encountered and we did not reach the river bottom until dark. I shall never forget the procession back to camp with the native hunters carrying bamboo torches, the dogs at their heels and the *bei shung* skin on the back of one of them. There was something virtually romantic about it, and it seemed to be the end of a dream, one of the few dreams that actually come true. I was only sorry that Anne did not have the opportunity to shoot the animal with us as she had worked harder on small animals and birds than either of us as well as doing a good share of difficult hunting without luck.

We planned to go up the next day and take the carcass and viscera down for preservation, thus making our contribution to science. Several scientific papers eventually emanated from the first dead specimen of a panda preserved in its entirety.

The panda reminded me more of a prehistoric animal than any living mammal I knew. The tremendous development of the masseter chewing muscles of the jaw-bones were a conspicuous adaptation to her diet of bamboo. She never accelerated her pace of walking even with all the loud talking, movement of men, and harrassment by dogs, behavior I could not imagine with a bear. A bear brought to bay by dogs will usually run off immediately if a man approaches. I have hunted bears and wild boar and even when wounded their first reaction is to get away. Neither in this case nor on November 16 when I observed two pandas pursued by dogs did the animal break into any kind of a run. Their limbs are so short and heavy, again a fine adaptation to their environment, they seem incapable of speed but probably can travel a great distance in one day through the bamboo jungle. The stomach contents of this female contained only bamboo stalks and some leaves.

Any truly alert or wild animal such as a leopard or even bear could have sensed our presence on the ridge at least before it came within ten feet of us! It seemed almost inexplicable but it was possible that the panda was frightened badly by the dogs and wanted to get away as rapidly as possible. I also have come to believe the giant panda is somewhat nocturnal and, like an owl disturbed in his daytime rest, she might have been a little stunned by daylight, but this seemed doubtful.

That day, as on November 16, the dogs were right on her heels and obviously did not have to exert themselves to keep up. After the last few weeks I considered that for so large an animal the giant panda was not a rare animal in this region.

It certainly was satisfying to collect an animal almost unknown in the outside world and one we had searched for for so long.

The next day Dean and Anne decided to carry out their plan of going for the night up to the woodcutter's lean-to in which I had spent two nights in the middle of November. They left shortly after lunch and I spent the afternoon working on the panda skin.

Later in the afternoon two coolies came in with Wong, whom we had sent to bring in the panda carcass and all the viscera. I believed the latter should be of great interest as up to that time none had ever been examined by scientists; it might prove of great value in determining whether the giant panda should be classified with the bears or raccoons.

Ho came in late in the afternoon with four of a species of bluebird and a titmouse. The former are lovely birds and of a deeper, richer hue of blue than any of our native birds of this genera. They occur in Chengwei in large flocks and seemed to be quite common at that time of year.

In the evening I cut off a piece of sirloin steak from the panda carcass and mashed it up, making a hamburger. It was not gamey tasting meat, was very bland, but entirely edible.

Before Dean and Anne had left the evening before, I proposed that in the morning I go up the Chengwei Valley with the hunters and their dogs and start them up the bamboo slope below the large field where Anne and Dean would be posting in case the dogs drove any animals to the field edge.

I arose very early and had finished breakfast half an hour before dawn. The usual delay was met with in waiting for the three hunters and their dogs to get assembled. I took Ho with me also.

At 7:00 A.M. we started up the Chengwei tributary, and this was my last tramp up this familiar stream. We walked an hour to a spot where two days ago we left the river to climb the east slope where we found the panda.

I left the men to ascend the opposite slope below the large field where Dean and Anne were posting. I longed to go up with them for a last hunt but there was work to do in camp because of our final departure from Chengwei the next day.

I paused once or twice to survey the familiar slopes with my glasses more for the sake of one final glimpse than any hope of spotting anything.

Returning to camp I had a busy morning measuring and labelling specimens and packing them in cases for traveling. During the morning a Tsapei hunter brought in a yearling ram blue sheep; I hardly recognized it because of the extremely long hair which it had grown to contend with the winter weather on the peaks.

Shortly after lunch Dean and Anne came in, having had no luck. The dogs had run a musk deer which they only caught a glimpse of.

I spent the greater part of the afternoon packing the large skins, rolling the greener ones in salt. All the skeletons, skulls etc. were packed too in preparation for leaving in the morning.

Bridge on Min River

Chapter Eleven

Our departure and narrow escape from bandits

WE departed from Chengwei on December 11. For the last time we looked up the tributary to the beautiful Chiung Lai Shan range at the head.

I walked rapidly along Chengo Creek to Tsapei, where we stopped to rest. The route from Tsapei down the main Chengo stream had not been traversed before, since we came in over the mountain from Tsaopo. The trail was fairly rough, going up and down and around cliffs, bordering the stream and keeping to the south side.

I was struck at how rapidly the vegetation seemed to change as we descended; the country began to appear more settled and I missed the colors of early autumn. It looked more arid and barer and was not cold.

In two hours from Tsapei we reached the Lliang Ho Do, (the junction of two rivers) where a large branch flowed in from the northeast.

As usual our night quarters were chosen on the roof. Our trail the next morning left the river bottom about six miles from the junction of the Tsaopo River and the main Chengo River and cut up on the intervening mountain ridges where I had spent so many interesting and enjoyable days.

Birds were abundant. Crows and magpies were extremely common while we occasionally saw water pippits and cinnamon sparrows.

After walking two hours we reached the crest of the mountain above the Min River valley, the identical spot where three months before we gazed for the first time at the realm of the giant panda, takin and blue sheep.

I found Anne and Dean waiting there, and it was truly glorious to sit in the bright sunlight and see for the last time the country we had become so familiar with. Up the Tsaopo River could be seen the ridges running up to the Chiung Lai Shan, while to the west I could see the forks at Lliang Ho Do and beyond the snow peaks above Chengwei to the Mamogo Valley.

As we started down the mountain to the Min River it was with the feeling of utmost regret and reluctance that I left behind probably forever a region so interesting in its animal life and beautiful in its scenery.

In less than an hour we had reached the river bottom at Siachow, where we found Don and Fung waiting for us. We were pleased to learn that Fung had purchased twenty more skins including one female golden monkey, five tufted deer, a serow and two small wildcats. We learned that the hunter Kao, to whom we had lent our spare rifles, had turned into a crack shot and according to Don had brought down a goral at four hundred and fifty yards. He had shot sixteen goral altogether and said he wounded a leopard on the high cliffs above the river but the animal fell into the river and was not recovered. Considering the precipitousness of the cliffs and the heavy rapids this was not at all unlikely.

We crossed the river by a ferry made of a few logs lashed together and propelled by pulling on a bamboo rope to which the raft was attached by a sliding wooden ring.

The first night we left Siachow we gave a banquet for our hunters and other mountain helpers who still accompanied us. In the preceding weeks individual characteristics of these hardy mountain men had become familiar to all of us. They continuously seemed to have an even temperament; surliness, anger, disrespect, moodiness never were apparent to us. We met with nothing but cheer, warmth, cooperativeness and even emotional ties from these people. For example, the Sages took Wong to Chengtu; as he stood at the airfield where they were boarding their plane to return to the other side of the world tears streamed down Wong's face—eloquent testimony of his love of this couple and the feeling he would never see them again.

Wong was an able hunter, the most courteous and cooperative of any of them. He was thoughtful while afield and worked assiduously for our comfort in camp. He never had to be told what to do. A tall handsome man, he was never austere and possessed a subtle sense of humor. He obviously commanded the respect of all the other mountain men.

Kao came nearest to being the aristocrat of our group. As the nephew of the former prince of Wassu he considered himself the most knowledgeable and most authoritative hunter. Mr. Fung, our interpreter, often told us Kao was a "very important man" in Wassu. He was ebullient, full of fun, and usually the center of conversation. At the same time he was a keen hunter and a crack shot. His features were more aquiline than most of the other mountain people and probably more characteristic of the original Chiang tribe.

Ho, who was with me much of the time, was a lovable man—always smiling. Although not as intelligent as Wong or Kao he was the most capable skinner and collector. We often lent him a shotgun for collecting birds and mammals. He was a fair hunter—not as capable as Kao or Wong.

These three men were with one or another of us the whole trip.

The hunter Tang was with us in the latter part of the expedition. A very small man with pigtails and a heavy opium smoker, he was as tough as a hickory nut and would scramble up mountains all day carrying a fifteen-pound muzzle loading gun and leading two dogs on chains. He was the most primitive of the mountain people we met and quite obviously was primarily a hunter, mountaineer, and woodsman.

These mountain people usually wore straw sandals even in winter but wrapped their legs and feet with coarse wool puttees. Many wore relatively long quilted coats and turbans for head covering.

Throughout the period in the mountains I wore woollen underwear, a flannel shirt and a water resistant wool jacket, a waterproof hat and "raintite" canvas trousers. I wore Indian moccasins with heavy wool socks and miner's rubbers. We all used four pronged iron cleats tied on our insteps.

The trip out to Kwanshien retraced our route of September.

Bird life was abundant; we observed many of the water redstarts, titmice, wagtails, magpies, crows, buzzards, as well as two cormorants flying up the valley close to the surface of the stream.

We saw two Tibetans en route for loads of tea. These men were very striking and picturesque in appearance. Their faces showed great strength and even fierceness, while they had a darker complexion than the average Chinese; their carriage was very erect and their walk distinct from the Chinese. They dressed in high Tibetan boots which must have been very warm and were probably absolutely necessary in their own country north and west of Sungpan. They carried Tibetan wool coats but wore them only over one shoulder. One had a grotesque large earring.

Natives informed us that a valley coming in from the east was a favored habitat of golden monkey and that a band of nearly a hundred had recently been observed there. Ten miles below Siachow was another valley coming in from the west which is called the *yea gnu* valley and apparently was a good place for takin.

Many skins were seen along the road and included leopard, monkey of a different species from golden, goral, tufted deer, musk deer, and badger. There were two live monkeys at different towns as well as a live goral and a young black bear. We arrived at Kwanshien on December 14 without incident and proceeded the next morning by automobile to Chengtu.

Dean and Anne left Chengtu for home by plane on December 20. Don and I stayed until December 31 collecting birds and mammals on the plain. Among the birds were the little blue kingfisher, white

Two Tibetans in Min River Valley

heron, green woodpecker, grey wagtail, water pippit, laughing thrush, redstart, shrike, tree sparrow, and ruddy sparrow.

I took one three-day trip to Cave Mountain, forty miles north of Chengtu, and collected seventy-five horseshoe bats in a limestone cave.

Carter and I left Chengtu on the afternoon of December 31 and boarded a sampan at Kiating on the Min River to proceed by boat to Suifu; there the Min empties into the Yangtze River and we would proceed thence by steamer to the coast. The trip was monotonous except for one incident where we might have lost all our equipment and all our specimens which were loaded on the boat. The boat was manned by four coolies and was about forty feet long. There was a bamboo covering where we could set up our cots and eat our meals. Jim, Don, and myself were together and the boat was owned by a lady of about thirty-two who was also aboard, and she was accompanied by a girl nine years old who was going downstream to be sold, as she told us, to a Chinese family down the river somewhere. There were four coolies manning the oars.

This trip to Suifu usually took five to six days in high water but we departed in extremely low water, and it took us seventeen days to travel to the Yangtze. Customarily we traveled by day and tied up at towns at night. Heavy fog often prevented an early departure in the morning.

On the morning of January 9 we were waiting at a town some seventeen miles below Kiating, postponing leaving until the fog lifted. We were hailed by a Chinese man drinking tea in a tea-house just above the river bank. I called back jokingly, returning his salutation of the morning, "Hao bu hao." I was surprised to have him come right down to the boat and demand a ride down river. On closer observation neither Don nor I liked his looks. He proferred some letter as an alleged "pass," but Jim, who thought he was a "bad man," told him we were sorry, but we could not take him. He seemed somewhat insistent and arrogant but finally departed—warning us of robbers downstream. We learned he was a scout for a group of bandits down-river, walking at night on trails beside the river, sleeping by day on any boat he could get a ride on, thus informing the band in advance of boat cargoes on the way downstream.

We had heard rumors of bandits for several days but nothing definite. That night we stopped at a large town fifty miles below Kiating, where we sent Jim to call on the magistrate with our cards. This official advised Jim it was better to turn back, for there was trouble below. Of course we could not consider this, as there was no definite news of bandits, and it would be foolish after so many days of slow struggle through low water to turn back on the grounds of a mere rumor and thus delay our return to Shanghai by almost a month. We left early the next morning and, although held up two hours by fog, proceeded over thirty miles. We stopped at a small town on the east bank for the night fifty miles north of Suifu and within a single day's travel. Since we had usually been one of the last boats leaving the towns each morning I aroused the coolies early and we were the first boat to leave. It was therefore with somewhat a sigh of relief—after so many days of delay—to get off early. Don and I arose a little before 8 A.M. for breakfast and during the next twenty minutes occurred the incident which undoubtedly saved all the material results of our trip as well as all the equipment.

We were just passing a flat river bar where a flock of ducks were resting seventy yards from the boat. Don decided to try a shot with buckshot from the shotgun and as he fired one duck dropped—wounded, but swimming. We were in a fast stretch of water and could not bring the boat up to the bank until we had drifted two hundred yards below the duck. Don got out to look for it, and, since he had to walk upstream some distance, we were delayed for twenty minutes. During this time three or four large junks passed us, and the nearest was one hundred yards ahead when we pushed off again.

An hour later we were just approaching a long island. The main channel of the stream was apparently on the west side; here the river was narrow and swift, sweeping out of sight around a bend in the island. On the east side there appeared to be plenty of relatively calm water; the river was broad but seemed to narrow down to a doubtful channel at the end of the island.

Just as we were opposite the upper end of the island shots were heard ahead around the bend where two junks ahead had disappeared. The men yelled "robbers." The large sampan ahead scented danger too late, as it was in the main sweep of the current; as it disappeared out of sight below the bend we saw the men frantically rowing for shore failing to make it and we heard more shots.

Then followed a few moments of excitement on our boat. We were safely in the other channel on the east side of the island but as yet had no idea of the exact location or number of the bandits. We began to prepare for trouble, and, while Jim and Don hurriedly unscrewed the rifles, I piled two sacks of rice up on the fore-deck as a protection and vantage point to shoot from.

All this time we were moving steadily along not far from the bank of the island. My rifle had two vaseline rags in each end of the barrel, and, since I had no ramrod at that moment to eject them, I loaded the magazine of Anne's rifle. Just then I saw several men with rifles running along the top of the bank some seventy-five yards off and assumed they were the robbers. The little girl on board was standing just behind the rice bags and as I pushed her inside I yelled to Don "Here they come." I was just preparing to draw a bead on one gun,

Sampan pulled into shore when Carter and the author retrieved a duck

although I did not intend to shoot unless one of them shot first, when Jim yelled they were the "police" in retreat. This was somewhat of a relief at the time, but the danger did not seem past yet—far from it.

We landed on the island where a long bar ran out from the shore, and there was no danger of approach by any bandits under cover. Jim walked back a short distance to confer with the police, who were just boarding a small boat heading for the opposite shore. Jim came back much excited with the story that there were three or four hundred bandits and that we should start for the opposite bank immediately. The police reported they even had a machine gun. These officials were en route to telephone for reinforcements from below. They said that eight hundred soldiers had driven back four hundred bandits there but two days before, but the renegades had turned up again unexpectedly that morning.

There was one other boat in the same channel with us and we all returned to the opposite bank, where we waited—hearing a shot now and then as other boats coming down river fell into the same trap. As we found out later, these bandits had been informed of our boat by the scout we had refused passage to.

Don and I decided, in view of the reports, however exaggerated they might be, that the odds were heavily against us if we attempted to get by without stopping. Furthermore, our coolies had little to lose by going ashore, and if they kept rowing the boat they might lose their lives, so it was impossible to count on them. Our ammunition was very limited and a few shots from us might bring fatal consequences.

Therefore we decided not to shoot if there were many men but kept a couple of rifles handy in case only a small band tried to stop us. We hid some of our money and letters of credit, but left some on our persons. We wrote the numbers of the latter and our passports inside the boat.

The boat ahead was obviously going to try the channel ahead, as there appeared to be no robbers guarding it. We followed well behind, expecting to hear the boat in front of us fired upon. Gradually it passed the danger mark and we were just breathing a sigh of relief when our boat turned ends and almost came to disaster in some rapids along the rocky bank not a quarter of a mile below the robbers, but we went safely past and were on our way once more with no one hurt, nothing lost, and a good scare. We saw one bandit standing on the west bank.

We reached Suifu that night and later some of the robbed boats came in. The bandits had stolen all the money, personal goods, and clothes worth taking. Undoubtedly had we not been warned by the shots which were fired at the junk ahead of us (when Don was in

Hunter Tang with muzzle-loading gun and two hunting dogs

pursuit of the duck), they would have rifled us of everything on the boat including the clothes on our backs. They had asked all the boats where the "foreign" boat was.

The latest reports stated there were probably only between fifty and a hundred robbers with about thirty guns including a machine gun. This was probably nearer the truth than the first report, but at the time there was no way of knowing the facts, and we had to act on the report we got. What a lucky day!

We returned to Shanghai by steamer; I arrived in New York March 15 via the Trans-Siberian Railroad and the Atlantic.

Chapter Twelve

Summary of the behavior and status of the giant panda

S I N C E extensive studies have been made of morphological characteristics of giant pandas, on how they ressemble or differ from
bears, raccoons, and the little red panda, the conflicting conclu-
sions reached by eminent zoologists will not be discussed in this
section. The most intensive study reference would be the work of
D.D. Davis published in 1964 and listed with other references in
the bibliography.

The focus of this chapter is what we know of the differences in
behavior of pandas and bears in the wild—clues to where one might
place them in the animal kingdom.

PALEONTOLOGICAL HISTORY

The evolution of the giant panda is as controversial as its classification and has been discussed in detail by Morris, Perry, Collins et al. The ancient Miacids living sixty million years ago were
the progenitors of most of the carnivores. Whether the small red
panda and giant panda sprung from the branches producing raccoons
or bears is purely speculative at present.

Granger of the American Museum of National History uncovered
fossil records of a type of giant panda, indicating the ancestors of the
giant panda millions of years ago once were widespread across large
areas of the east Asian and Indian continent. Granger discovered
well-preserved skulls and skeleton bones in Pleistocene sediments
of the Yangtze River near Wanshien in Szechwan. Ernst Schäfer
believes the fossil giant pandas belonged to a different family, since
the ancient panda remains were from a much larger animal than the
present day giant panda.

GEOGRAPHICAL RANGE

Pandas have been found in most of western Szechwan Province on
the east side of the mountains separating Tibet from the plains of

Szechwan. They occur as far north as Kansu Province and Sowerby reported evidence of giant pandas in Shensi Province, a report recently confirmed by Chinese workers. H.C. Pen, a Chinese zoologist, observed pandas in Tibet, extending the potential range two hundred miles north and west of earlier records.

Many mammals near the perimeter of their normal home ranges may wander. E. W. Nelson (1918), who worked in the field in Mexico for fourteen years, comments on the North American jaguar (*Felis hernandesi*): "Few predatory animals are such wanderers as the Jaguar, which roams hundreds of miles from its native home, as shown by its occasional appearance far within our borders (U.S.A.)."

When mountain lions (*Felis cougar*) were extirpated from their ancestral range in eastern North America almost one hundred years ago a small nucleus survived in New Brunswick, Canada and the Everglades in Florida. In recent years the Canadian zoologist, B. Wright, has documented instances of lions wandering between these two areas. An instance well documented is the occurrence of the mountain lion in the Great Smoky Mountains of North Carolina, hundreds of miles north of the Everglades.

It is possible that Pen's observation was of pandas simply wandering; as he points out, they were still close to mountain country. His record is the first of sighting pandas or their sign in Tibet in spite of the many travelers who have passed through this section of that country. Perry has reported new (1966) sightings of giant pandas in the hills north of Sining, several miles northeast of Oring Nur, but gives no details on who observed them, what time of year they were seen, or how many were seen. These could have been in Kansu Province, parts of which are recognized panda habitat.

The account by Pen raises some puzzling questions. How could an observer even with a telescope identify at over two miles several varieties of vegetation the panda was eating? Furthermore, it seems to me highly unlikely that the cubs "followed and suckled their mother as does a little pig or a calf." Most land carnivores suckle their young from a prone position. Also, other evidence cited in this same chapter suggests that cubs become independent of their mother once they are old enough to travel and start eating bamboo.

One other scrap of conflicting testimony comes from the Chinese giant panda zoo-keepers in Peking. They observed that the mother panda habitually holds one cub under one forearm next to her body and can readily move around on three legs for feeding. When twins were born in captivity in China one died, since the mother could only carry one at a time. The Chinese therefore hypothesize that in the wild a mother giant panda can only raise one cub.

It is possible there is a problem of semantics in Pen's article so some of these questions can only be answered by intensive field studies.

These Tibetan observations raise the intriguing possibility that finally the giant panda, like the takin and serow, originally isolated in western Szechwan in the Pleistocene, has begun to extend its geographical range.

Perry concluded that the vicinity of Tatsienlu and western areas are part of the stronghold of the panda but Schäfer wrote me as follows in 1974: "Tatsienlu is certainly *not* the center of panda range but possibly its westernmost boundary." Schäfer hunted in the bamboo jungles there for fourteen days in 1931 and thirty days in 1934 "without finding any sign of panda whatsoever." The presence of skins of panda in a town or trade route is no proof that the panda occurs there. Skins from panda country have often been recorded from markets in Chengtu, one hundred miles from panda country and thirty miles east of the nearest mountains.

I suspect the range of the panda is spotty. The evidence gathered from reported sightings and the sites of captured or killed pandas seem to leave little doubt that the main range of pandas is in the Wassu country where many of the live pandas have come from and where we saw so much sign.

The first Westerner entering the part of Wassu we visited was H. Weigold in 1914. It was "rediscovered" in 1931 by Brooke Dolan. Schäfer has informed me that Weigold, who accompanied Dolan and Schäfer unsuccessfully, attempted to have Dolan bypass the area on the basis it was too steep and rugged to attempt.

HOME RANGE

Daily and seasonal travels of the true bears are usually determined by different seasonal sources of food. In the early spring just after emerging from hibernation grizzly bears often frequent the grasslands above timber, where they eat wild celery or dig out ground squirrels or marmots. They are particularly adept at catching the squirrel. I have observed these bears traveling on talus slopes under precipitous cliffs frequented in winter by mountain goats or mountain sheep. Often these ungulates are killed in snow slides or accidents, and the bears sometimes find dead animals. They eat carrion as well as fresh meats. In coastal regions the large brown bears, cousins of the grizzlies, have well-beaten trails beside salmon streams where they congregate during the spawning runs of these fish. The bears are skillful fishermen, wading deeply in the rapids and often snapping up fish underwater. Black bears will also visit salmon streams in the fall. In other parts of their range black bears congregate in blueberry fields, abandoned apple orchards or beechnut ridges, where they gorge on these fruits.

All North American species of bears will congregate at garbage dumps within their range, demonstrating they are in every sense omnivorous feeders, and opportunistic in seeking the most available foods. Without access to artificial food sources, such as garbage dumps, which receive new disposals every day, bears must travel widely to fulfill their energy needs to prepare for hibernation late in the fall.

Bears need to accumulate large layers of fat to survive the winter in hibernation or nurse cubs. Since bears are not true hibernators, like marmots, ground squirrels, or jumping mice, they do not become as completely dormant as the latter and can be aroused from a winter den. Their respiration slows but they unquestionably need more energy to survive than the hibernating rodents. The cubs are about the same relative size at birth as those of the giant panda and are born in mid-winter and usually capable of traveling with the mother soon after she emerges from her winter den.

If a bear bred in the early spring, as sometimes occurs with the giant panda, the cubs would be born in early fall at the time a bear ordinarily would be feasting on its most available food to prepare for retirement in winter. The cubs would be old enough to leave the den in mid-winter but they could not survive. Most bears in the north breed in late June or July and the cubs are born in mid-winter. Therefore this seasonal pattern of the bear is obviously an adaptation for survival and successful reproduction.

I suspect that if not disturbed, a single panda, compared to a bear, is relatively local in home range. The large male I tracked on November 12 made almost a complete circle where his track was finally lost below snow line but had not traveled more than a half a mile from where I picked up his track in the morning. A track of similar size had been found on November 5 in almost the precise place I had found the fresh trail on November 12. Of course there is no way of telling whether this was the same animal, but there were sections in these panda mountains after snowfall where one could expect to find fresh panda sign not more than two or three days old on every daily visit. I speculate that such stretches of country were frequented daily by one or more pandas. A rough estimate of home range of any one panda would be five to seven square miles of land surface. The horizontal map measurement would be less in such a precipitous country.

There is one other possibility conceivably pertinent in measuring the delineation of home range. Some large predators such as the mountain lion in western America have been studied exhaustively by capturing, tagging, attaching radio transmitters, and other methods of measuring territory, home range, and behavior. Regardless of availability of prey, mountain lions are spaced by apparently sociological factors. They range and live in certain tracts. There is some overlapping but some spacing appears a factor in their population density. I have found much the same phenomenon in wild bobcats of the northeastern United States. We found by tagging with radio transmitters that once young cats become independent of their mother they tend to disperse widely.

Whereas a normal home range of an adult bobcat might be five square miles we found one half-grown kitten moving thirty miles in about forty-eight hours in one instance.

Whether there is any such behavior in the giant panda is unknown but could be determined by other studies suggested in this chapter.

LOCAL POPULATIONS

After snow had fallen I believed I could conservatively make a minimum count of pandas occupying the Chengo Valley and its tributaries in an area of about seventy square miles, only a fraction of which we were able to investigate. From November 12 the Chengo Valley was covered with sufficient snow to detect pandas crossing from one main range to another. We continually traversed the valley from the Chengwei fork to the headwaters of the Chengo stream at timber line.

Two pandas were sighted on November 16 on the west side of Chengwei Valley. I shall assume the large male I tracked November 12 was one of these. On December 8, when we shot the female on the east side, there was also a track of a smaller panda. I have assumed one of these pandas was separate from the pandas seen November 16. A third large panda was chased very high on December 7 but could have been one seen previously.

A small giant panda climbed a tree in Tsapei earlier in the fall and the hunters saw a small panda, assumed to be the same one, in a tree six miles west of Tsapei at a later date.

From five to ten miles north three pandas, based on location, time, and size of tracks, were present in Mamogo Valley and at least one present to the west in Dabeishuigo Valley. I believe there were eight pandas, or one per ten square miles, known to be present, but my conservative estimate of pandas occupying this area would be between twenty and thirty. Subsequent to our visit Captain H. C. Brocklehurst and Quentin Young shot three pandas from the area and most of the live pandas including those caught by Mrs. Ruth Harkness and Floyd Smith came from this region.

The age structure of the animals known to be present was not indicative of a thriving population. There must have been very young pandas either nursing or confined to a restricted area beacuse of deep snow. We found no very small tracks.

Two additional pandas were killed in trees by natives on the perimeter of the area we investigated. We probably covered little more than twenty square miles of the region when snow conditions were favorable for track counts. I believe the Chengwei tributary alone at that time was inhabited by six or seven pandas. For a mammal this size the population I have estimated in that area at that time suggests abundance.

I am unaware of the status today but the numbers we observed or estimated might well provide a yardstick against which to measure changes in the population in the heart of the giant panda range.

PANDA FEEDING HABITS

I have emphasized that the bears of the northern regions of North America are omnivorous and travel widely in search of food, but the giant panda has no such requirement to ensure survival. The panda is chiefly herbivorous and his principal source of food is bamboo, a plant growing densely with fresh green leaves and stalks throughout the year. Some authors proclaim the pandas only eat "bamboo shoots" or "bamboo roots." We found they ate large stalks as readily as leaves or smaller shoots but found no evidence of feeding on roots.

One remarkable physical attribute of the panda is a prehensile sixth "claw" on his front paws. These act like a hand. He can grasp a bamboo stalk and pull it down.

No details have been provided by Perry or Pen and more recent Chinese authors on their general statement that pandas eat mammals. I am not doubting these observers and will only state that during the fall and early winter in Wassu I examined hundreds of droppings and found no evidence of predation on small mammals. Even the pile of droppings I found above tree line only contained the remains of bamboos.

The two captive pandas acquired in 1972 in the National Zoological Park in Washington have between them killed one bird and two mice at time of writing. In each instance they did not attempt to eat their prey. Of course zoo pandas are generally well fed.

The number of small mammals we trapped and our observations on snow in panda country attest to the availability and abundance of small mammals if pandas were adept at catching them.

In some instances the conspicuous droppings (four inches to six inches long and two inches to three inches in diameter) contained only leaves. Zoo female pandas in breeding condition were found to eat leaves and very small stalks, so this may be a clue. The female shot in December had droppings of stalks mixed with some leaves.

Whereas I have followed trails of grizzlies or black bears in late fall and found diggings, logs torn apart, or stones overturned, I never saw any such signs on panda trails. I would not doubt that the panda might be as opportunistic as any other carnivore in his feeding but doubt if in his wild state the giant panda depends for energy on small mammals or birds. Certainly in the winter, when the conditions are the most rigorous, one might expect to find evidence of their hunting small mammals. Père David suspected they lived on flesh in winter. Many small mammals foraged on top of the snow. I saw voles and others on the forest floor when there was no snow but saw no indications pandas either hunted or caught them. Pandas apparently don't dig.

I never found that the panda ate any one bamboo patch clear. They seemed to wander in a zigzag pattern, cropping a stalk here and another there so that there were no "eaten-out" patches within the bamboo jungle. There have been several references in other literature to "tunnels" in the bamboos used by panda. I often found game trails running up ridges used by all the wild species in the area but few that suggested "tunnels." While feeding, the panda wanders all over the mountain slopes. Since the bamboo emerges in the feces in an almost undigested state the pandas must spend a great deal of time in feeding and eat large quantities to get sufficient nourishment. The panda trailed November 12, where the track was found early in the morning, deposited at least between eighty and ninety droppings over two or three miles of its trail. There were an additional thirty droppings at its bed where I jumped the animal.

The farmers in the cradle of the best panda mountains spoke only of pandas raiding beehives in the honey season. They said their vegetable crops and corn were chiefly damaged by wild boar.

I do not doubt wild panda will sample bulbs and other herbs but it would be hardly necessary to migrate to the Tibetan steppes as Pen suggests to seek these foods when they could find an even richer assortment by climbing two thousand feet plus or minus above bamboos to the nutritious vegetation of their local grasslands. Panda droppings, so relatively undigested, persist for many weeks after deposit. With the exception of the one group I found a thousand feet above timber no others were found during three weeks roaming the grassland country. None were found in the same area in April and May by the Dolan expedition in 1931.

There may be other herbs or woody vegetation they eat in the farmlands just below the bamboos, an area they often travel through, even though we found that droppings in these areas also only contained bamboo.

In spite of the demonstration by zoos that pandas can be weaned to a variety of foods, their great masseter muscles and powerful crunching teeth must have evolved as an adaptation chiefly to eat bamboos. H. C. Raven (1936) listed the following panda anatomical features as typical of animals with a specialized herbivorous diet: the extremely horny linings of the esophagus, the thick-walled muscular and elongated stomach, the proportionately small-sized liver, the comparatively small size of the gall bladder (presumably associated with more continuous feeding), the large size of the pancreas, and the elongation of the jeguno-ileum.

BREEDING HABITS

We carefully examined the carcass of the female adult panda we collected December 8 and there was little evidence of fat accumulation so typical of bears at this season. If the pandas in the wild have two breeding seasons I can't see how either season could be a disadvantage for successful rearing of cubs. Even in mid-winter a female could briefly leave her den and fill up on bamboos readily available outside any lair. Back-dating the ten pandas of known age (based on weight) listed by Morris and using 140 days as the gestation period, cubs would have been born in January, February, May, June, October and November. Conception would have occurred every month but November, December, July, and August. We found two pandas traveling together November 16, suggesting breeding may occur in November. These data are partly speculative. A further point of interest in breeding habits is that zoo pandas back up to various objects and scrape off strong scent from anal glands when they are "in season." I have found no evidence of such behavior in wild bears.

HIBERNATION

We found tracks in twelve inches of snow at temperatures close to 0°F. on the Chengo stream watershed on December 5, and many other tracks in snow. The statements by the native hunters, and our own observation, seem convincing evidence that giant pandas do not hibernate.

In a paper I published in 1938 and written before there were any data on zoo pandas I used the unfortunate adjective "stupid" referring to the giant panda. Every subsequent publication took me to task for this statement. In the same article I stated that compared to bears the panda is not alert. Even zoo people such as Desmond Morris state that they do not consider the giant panda "over intelligent."

It seems to me that the panda, like the bear, would fear above all its chief predator, man, since they have been hunted by man for hundreds of years. I saw behavior of pandas I could not imagine of bears, an animal as wild as any I know, except in national parks, where they have lost their fear of humans and in some instances when they are accompanied by cubs.

I cite four examples of panda behavior, one of which is hearsay. One was the panda we shot. We had been yelling and moving around even after the panda appeared chased by dogs sixty yards away. Possibly because of confusion and the worrying of the dogs the panda walked within ten feet of Sage.

Another was a panda climbing a pine tree in open farmland in full view and within hearing of two farmhouses and permitting a native hunter to walk up a trail five hundred and fifty yards in the open and shoot at it from fifty yards before it climbed down a tree.

The missionary explorer D. C. Graham organized seventy hunters who caught two young pandas for gifts to the United States from Madam Chai. A sixty-pound male was caught by hand when pursued by dogs. I cannot imagine a young bear caught thus. The only damage to the capturer was torn clothing.

The hearsay story is that of a native woodchopper finding a panda in a tree in fairly thick cover and killing the panda with an axe as it tried to climb down.

Bears, particularly black bears, run at an amazing rate even with one whiff of human scent.

I have one record of a large brown bear on a north Pacific coast island bolting on smelling a human foot trail two hours old. I never saw a panda under stress travel faster than a leisurely walk, but zoo pandas seem capable of more rapid locomotion. I suspect that the panda's eyesight may be poor. The same can be said of the bears, although the latter are quick to detect movement. A bear has keen hearing and may be more sensitive to sound than pandas. Possibly the panda's sense of smell is its keenest sense. The panda's anal scent glands are apparently used for communication. The panda I jumped and trailed November 12 most possibly was roused by my scent, but the sense of hearing could have also played a part.

Chapter Twelve

Fully grown pandas vary in weight from two hundred and twenty to three hundred pounds, depending on sex. Most of our weight records are from zoo animals.

LONGEVITY

Zoo records of longevity may be misleading because of the artificiality of a confined environment. Several zoo pandas have lived for thirteen or fourteen years, but I suspect the life span may be longer in the wild.

INTELLIGENCE

The zoo pandas have great curiosity and perform unique antics, enthralling the public. An example would be pandas moving an object in their cages to a position where they could climb in an attempt to get out of a pen. The female Washington panda became very skillful at blocking the door of its pen to avoid being moved from the outside pen to the indoor section of it.

Giant pandas caught several months old from the wild show comparatively less fear of man than most carnivores. Most carnivores become tame if caught at a young enough age to become imprinted on their captors.

For example, I easily tamed a bobcat taken three weeks old just after its eyes were open but young cats six weeks old have become imprinted on their mother and never become tame. Giant pandas several months old taken captive do not cower in their cages. The Washington pandas even approach their keepers to have their backs scratched through the cage bars.

Could it be, in view of its twilight and nocturnal habits, that the panda, like the owl, is dazed by bright lights? As far as I know this doesn't appear true of captive pandas.

PACE

The ordinary gait of a panda is walking with head held low and the front feet pigeon toed. If they hurry they do not gallop like bears but place the front and hind paws on the same side on the ground together, giving them a pace not unlike a horse pacing. From somewhat cursory observation it seemed to me that, when walking, the panda does not break its wrist with every step as is customary with bears.

The commonest sound made by a panda is a birdlike bleat, a very light note for such a large mammal. I heard a loud growl of a panda worried by dogs. Some workers and natives have reported the males roar in breeding season.

RESTING PLACES

I found many giant panda nests under the cover of ledges on the precipitous cliffs, at bases of trees, and under a stump in one place. I found a good many caves several feet long cutting into the side of the mountains, but found no panda sign in these. Apparently they prefer to rest in more open places. Resting areas in deep snow at the base of trees in cold weather attests to the insulation of their fur. Deeper recesses may be sought by a mother with a newborn cub but we didn't find any sign of newborn animals. When the panda has taken the trouble to bite off bamboo stalks and arrange them in a circular bed under a ledge it suggests possible areas for bringing forth young. The natives reported young were often produced among the cliffs.

COLORATION

I doubt if the color of the giant panda is cryptic or has any survival advantage. Giant pandas are conspicuous in the open but are usually in cover at twilight or night. Since they are most commonly abroad in the dark, color would not be important. The vulnerable prey of the bamboo belt—musk deer, muntjac deer, tufted deer, goral, serow and young wild boar—have coats of somber or dark color.

CARE OF CUBS

There is one other aspect of panda behavior which somewhat puzzled me. Whereas female bears are often accompanied by their cubs for two years I never found a panda track followed by a small track of a cub. The young cub that Schäfer shot did not appear to be accompanied by his mother. Of course when the panda is as young as the one that Mrs. Harkness found it is accompanied by an adult; at least there was an adult right close to the den, presumably the mother. It is quite possible that the young pandas become independent of their mother as soon as they are weaned and start eating bamboo. I never found a really small track of any pandas in this country, and there must have been some very young animals someplace in the area.

The young panda with a six-inch track we chased with dogs was not accompanied by an adult.

PREDATORS

The panda lived thousands of years successfully with natural predators before man appeared on the scene. Until dead pandas, and especially live ones, yielded a handsome sum to native hunters pandas apparently withstood human predation for hundreds of years. In fact, the natives prefer the skin of the blue sheep or a takin to that of a panda.

As reported by other authors, leopards and wild dogs might be the most important potential predators of panda. In ancestral times tigers might have been a possible predator on the fringes of the panda habitat. I doubt that the Himalayan black bear would have any occasion to prey on the panda; although often in panda country, he would be seeking a totally different type of food, and there is some question he could kill any but a very young panda. In my judgment the fierce wild dogs of Wassu could be the most serious potential predator. Pandas seem to show an ancestral fear of dogs. Su-Lin, the young panda found by Mrs. Harkness, was so terrified of the barking of dingoes in the next cage at the Brookfield Zoo that he had to be moved to another compartment, and so frightened subsequently of the smell of dogs at a farm in the country that he refused his food and moaned all night and had to be moved elsewhere.

I suspect only a young panda would be vulnerable to these dogs but the agility of the young *bei shung* to scramble up a tree could be a defensive mechanism. The best deterrent to wild dog–panda conflict is the great abundance of available ungulate prey in the giant panda range, thus acting as buffer species. There are high populations of serow, musk deer, tufted deer, wild boar, muntjac, goral (in cliffs), possibly young takin, and large numbers of small mammals. I have cited one instance of dogs killing a female serow and once we heard them running goral. Leopards are not very common in the belt of bamboos frequented by pandas. I found one dropping and a few tracks. We found many more leopard tracks above timber. Leopards were abundant in the vicinity of the Min River where they chiefly preyed on goral among the cliffs.

TEMPERAMENT

Although individual pandas differ in temperament, compared to most bears they are not savage carnivores. The panda seems more easy going and phlegmatic than a bear. The native dogs of Wassu are afraid of the Himalayan black bear and won't trail them but readily chase pandas. Although some pandas in zoos have demonstrated power in their forelegs as weapons, the panda we collected with dogs biting at it on all sides growled once and bit one dog in the foot; a black bear in the same position would have been bowling dogs all over the place with his forepaws. The native hunters have no fear of the panda but are apprehensive in close quarters with such a mammal as a bull takin.

TREE CLIMBING OF PANDAS

I suspect the frequency that pandas climb trees is overemphasized, although Perry believes otherwise.

However, Schäfer has a record of four pandas climbing trees in April. One was treed by his German roughhaired pointer. One of these was very small and he shot it. The others he described as adults but they were seen at a distance, when it would be difficult to judge whether the panda was fully grown.

We had three records of pandas climbing trees. All were near or amongst the farms, and all were small, about half-grown. The cub Schäfer shot out of a larch tree in 1931 still had milk teeth. It is possible that fully adult pandas seldom climb trees and may be like the grizzly bear, which can scramble up trees as a young cub but is unable to climb once it has attained adult weight; the black bears can climb at any age. We found two large spruce trees lying at a forty-degree angle unmistakably used by pandas. An adult could have walked up one of these. The young pandas thus would have a method of escape not possible for the adult. At least the zoo people refer to adult pandas as extremely clumsy climbers. The one half-grown panda I chased with dogs for at least forty minutes made no attempt to climb a tree and continued on foot after the dogs had left the trail. Although the natives said that on occasion their dogs treed a panda they did not seem to be too definite about this, and the several pandas we chased made no attempt to escape or to avoid the dogs by climbing.

THE FUTURE OF THE PANDA

Since the Chinese have successfully bred the panda in captivity, two cubs having survived out of ten born, and have established a sanctuary in the Min range northeast of the area we visited, there seems hope for the future of this endangered species. The local people are serflike, and I am sure they will abide by any laws imposed on them. My only concern is that if they are still allowed to set spear traps which they may claim are being set for takin, such traps are non-selective and may just as well kill a panda as a takin.

There are two dangers in my estimation for the giant panda. One is that if it continues to be a status symbol for zoos, and a political animal being given by China as a gift to various countries, there is some threat to the population. But as long as pandas born in captivity can be the source of future gifts, the wild population will not be threatened. The other chief danger is the extent of development in the panda country. I believe that according to recent maps there may be better roads into the country, but they have not yet penetrated the ruggedest mountains. According to one map there is a secondary road at least into the town of Wenchwan, whence it is an easy two- or three-day trip into the best part of the panda range. Although I found pandas relatively abundant in their habitat, the latter is restricted to a small geographical range.

FUTURE STUDY

I would suggest that a pilot study in one of the good panda valleys be instituted by zoologists or biologists from both China and the United States. The key to estimating populations is knowing what the home range is as well as the geographical range. One could use the methods which have proved so successful tracking some of the large predators in the United States. If pandas could be equipped with radio transmitters and receiving stations set up in strategic points one could start to determine the number and behavior of the animals in one particular valley. The techniques of using this electronic equipment are well developed and have proved successful with grizzly bears.

EXPENSE

Equipment alone would cost about three thousand dollars. The logistics of getting into the country and the labor of erecting proper receiving towers would be time consuming. Presumably we already have knowledge of a tranquilizer drug with which wild pandas could be injected so they could be handled. Although the Chinese have been fairly successful in capturing them I think a large number of bear foot snares as have been developed for the black bear in Oregon might be one effective way of catching them. The possible use of good hounds might at least be tried, since I feel persistent trailing by dogs of this type might well push a panda up a tree or in some type of refuge. Although expensive, it would be extremely helpful if a helicopter could be made available. Studying even one male and one female from one valley would be a fine opening wedge to our knowledge of the panda. The larger number of pandas that could be radio tagged, the more thorough our knowledge could be.

I truly believe that, if funds could be provided and the cooperation of the Chinese solicited, this study would be highly feasible and an insurance for the survival of the panda.

I would suggest a team of three United States biologists, at least one of whom is skilled in the use of electronics, and three or more Chinese zoologists, one of whom can act as interpreter.

Any estimate of cost of a one year study (the minimum time for even a pilot study) could be only rough. Counting all travel costs, equipment, labor, etc., I estimate a minimum starting figure should be forty thousand dollars. If it were a cooperative venture with China possibly the expenses could be shared.

I feel this book is a contribution to knowledge on the giant panda, but I am aware the surface has just been scratched in our knowledge about this remarkable beast in the wild.

Here is one of the few large mammals of the world relatively restricted in range. Of ancient lineage, the giant panda is the most fascinating large mammal I know of. As the symbol of the World Wildlife Fund, the giant panda would be an ideal subject for a cooperative scientific field study by Americans and Chinese.

Appendix I

Summary of ecology of life zones in panda country

FROM 16,000 to 17,000 feet above sea level E. H. Wilson characterized as an "alpine desert," with a few cushion herbs and a tiny species of primrose.

The alpine zone below 16,000 feet to timber line, occasionally visited by the giant panda, is mostly grassy meadows on steep slopes and cliffs with an infinite variety of herbs. We were in this area after the flowering season, but Wilson vividly describes carpets of various bright colored flowers in the late spring and summer. He characterizes the following as typical of these altitudes: primroses (*Primula* sp.), gentians (*Gentiana* sp.), orchids (*Cyprediuma* sp.), *Meconopsis, Compositae, Spiraea,* and dwarf juniper. Fumeworts (*Corydalis* sp.), for example, have 70 species and louseworts (*Pedicularis* sp.), have 100 species occurring in "countless thousands." There are 100 species of ragworts (*Senecio* sp.) and 90 species of gentians. There are many species of grasses.

Timber line in western China varies from 10,500 feet to 14,500 feet depending on exposure and rainfall. Therefore the same life zone on different slopes may vary 4,000 feet in altitude.

We only observed bird life in the alpine zone in October. There may well be several species that breed in this zone and migrate to either lower altitudes or to the south. There are some species occupying the high altitude throughout the year. Chief among these are some of the pheasants. The regal monal pheasant (*Lophophorus lhuysi*) was only found high above timber line like the ptarmigan of North American or Scandinavian mountains. The tragopan pheasant (*Tragopan temmincki*) is more a bird of timber line than of the grasslands or the peaks. Occasionally blood pheasants of a new race (*Ithaginis sinensis annae*) ventured to timber line but lived primarily in the bamboo life zone of lower altitudes. Other birds observed above timber line included snow pigeons (*Columbia leuconota gradaria*), rock buntings (*Emberiza eia* subsp.), ravens (*Corvus* sp.), hedge sparrows (*Prunella strophiata multistriata*), some unidentified larks, a kestrel falcon, and an unidentified large *Buteo* hawk.

There were far more mammals than birds in the alpine zone.

There is no well-defined food chain. The chief predator is the leopard (*Panthera pardus*).

It is possible the Chinese wild red dogs (*Cuon alpinus*), may occasionally hunt above timber but, in winter at least, we only found them preying on ungulates below timber line.

Another carnivore of the peaks is the red fox (*Vulpes v. hoolei*).

The primary prey of the leopards is the blue sheep (*Pseudois nagaar szechuanensis*), often occurring in herds of fifty or more. The blue sheep have massive skulls characteristic of goats. Some zoologists classify them with goats. They may be an ancestral progenitor of both goats and sheep.

Leopards probably also prey on the abundant voles (*Microtus* sp.), mouse-hares (*Ochotona* sp.), and possibly the monal pheasant in nesting season. The chief prey of the red fox must be the common vole and mouse-hare. It is also possible that some of the smaller wildcats in the region hunt above timber line. We observed some small cat tracks, either a small species or very young leopards.

The basic prey in the alpine zone are the very numerous small mammals. We trapped 270 small mammals of ten species in the three weeks spent on the peaks. Eighty-four of these were shrews, including shrew moles (*Uropsiles soricipes*), bi-colored shrews (*Sorex excelsis*), Asiatic long-tailed shrews (*Sorex h. hypsibia*), striped-back shrews (*Sorex c. cylindrica*), long-tailed brown shrews (*Sorex argatus sihalis*), and short-tailed shrews (*Blarinella quadriticauda*). The shrew moles are one of the mammal species confined to western Szechwan. Allen considered them very primitive and possibly forbears of both shrews and moles. Shrews are not ordinarily palatable to carnivores due possibly to the scent glands most species have, so may not contribute to a food chain.

The soil must be productive of many kinds of invertebrate fauna to support such a large number of insectivores.

The shrew mole is confined to timber line or just below the rhododendron zone. Only two species, the long-tailed brown shrew and the bi-colored shrew, were not caught at lower altitudes. Swan (1961), in studying the ecology of the high Himalayas, found some species of spiders and other invertebrates high above timber line. He found many insects at 16,000 feet and one species of spider at more than 20,000 feet. I have observed and caught shrews in shale and rock high above timber line and vegetation in the Canadian Rockies. The only prey I could find on cursory inspection was a large species of spider. I suspect that some of the two species of Chinese shrews that I found confined to the alpine zone may well range higher than any other mammal. Since I did not go above 15,000 feet I was unable to verify this. Three species of mice were found in this zone. The Asiatic wood mouse (*Apodemus* sp.) was confined to timber line. We

caught 141 voles from timber line to the highest peaks. The most
abundant mammal was a short-tailed brown vole (*Microtus ireni*
[Neoden]). A few long-tailed voles (*Microtus* sp.) were also captured.
One lagomorph, the pika, or mouse-hare (*Ochotona* sp.), was largely
confined to the high grasslands. Unlike the North American species
these little hares were rarely found in talus and rock piles but ranged
all over the grasslands.

The rhododendron life zone extended roughly for 2,000 feet below
timber line depending on exposures. In north-facing slopes it grew
well above the bamboo belt and seemed a hardy species. Most of the
rhododendrons were large twisted trees, but there must be more
than one species a discerning botanist could recognize. Wilson reports 160 species of rhododendrons, mostly in western China.

At least five species of spruce trees and white fir are scattered
throughout the rhododendron and bamboo forest extending to timber line.

Animal life was very scarce in the rhododendron belt during the
fall and winter. Shrew moles, Asiatic wood mice, and striped squirrels (*Tamiops* sp.) were found. A few large animals occasionally
wandered into the edges but there were no signs of feeding. As far as
we could tell pandas shunned this life zone. They must occasionally
pass through it, however, since the panda making the droppings I
found on September 28 above timber line had to walk through the
rhododendron belt.

The most important life zone in Wassu is the bamboo (*Sinarundi-
naria*) belt; depending on rainfall and exposure bamboo was found as
low as 6,000 feet and as high as 12,000 feet. The important feature to
recognize, especially in the Chengo Valley, where pandas and other
mammals were most abundant, was that, although bamboo was the
dominant plant, there were other shrubs, deciduous trees, and open
fields lending a variety of cover.

Wilson lists a large number of trees and woody vegetation species occurring in this region. Some of the more typical species are:
birches (*Betula* sp.), maples (*Acer* sp.), silver fir, hemlock, spruces,
pine (*Pinus armandi*), spiraea alder (*Alnus* sp.), several viburnums,
the varnish tree (*Rhus veyailiflua*), walnut (*Juglans regia*), several
kinds of poplar (*Populus* sp.) and willow (*Salix* sp.), larch (*L.
potaninii*), linden ((*Tilia* sp.), several species of Lauraceae, clematis
vine (*clematis montana*), several species of wild rose (*Rosa* sp.),
hornbeam (*Ostrya* sp.) and ash (*Fraxinus* sp.).

Open fields are scattered on some of the high slopes especially
around the farms. Brushy fields extend a thousand feet above the
houses, where they are invaded by tongues and patches of bamboo in
their upper reaches, areas often used by the *bei shung* (the Chinese
name for giant panda, meaning "white bear").

There was a great variety of birds throughout the late fall and early winter. The most abundant birds were the laughing or jay thrushes. We collected or observed the following species of these thrushes: the barred (*Garrulax lunutata*), the ashy (*G. einerlea cinericaps*), the black-faced (*G. affinis blythii*) and Elliot's (*G. ellioti ellioti*). Other common species were two kinds of babblers, the golden-breasted (*Alcippe chrysatis swinoii*) and the grey-headed (*Alcippe cinerciceps cinerciceps*). Wagtails were common. Two kinds were seen, the white (*Motacilla alba hodgsoni*) and the grey (*Motacilla cinerea*).

Blood pheasants were extremely abundant in the bamboos, often occurring in large flocks.

The common names of less abundant birds included several species of tits, at least four species of woodpeckers, two species of redstarts, three kinds of dippers, nutcrackers, nuthatches, golden pheasant and koklass pheasant, ring-necked pheasant, a snipe, bulbuls, many other thrushes, wrens, chats, and several others. The complete list of this collection is in Appendix 3.

It is conjectural how many of these were migrants. The pheasants and titmice probably stayed all winter and possibly several of the other species. We left the area December 12, presumably after migration, when the species mentioned above were still present.

I believe we observed or collected a good sample of mammals in this zone. The giant panda, according to Allen, is the only large mammal in the area not extending its ancestral range widely to the west and southwest in the foothills of the main Himalayas. We found the panda relatively common. Most occur in the Chengwei Valley, where three were seen and sign was everywhere. They were also common further west on the tributaries of the main Chengo stream. Other large mammals were takin (*Budorcas taxicolor thibetana*), serows (*Capricornis milne edwardsi*), leopard (*Felis pardus*), goral (*Naemorhedus griseus*), muntjac deer (*Muntiacus muntjac*), musk deer (*Moschus machiferus*), tufted deer (*Elaphodus cephalodus*), wild red dog (*Cuon alpinus*), golden monkey (*Rhinopithecus roxellanae*), lesser red panda (*Ailurus fulgens*), wild boar (*Susmoupinensis*), and Himalayan black bear (*Soleriarctos thibetanus*). One other large predator, the Chinese tiger, (*Felis tigris ariolensis*), is very rare in the Wassu country. Weigold recorded one killed in the Min River valley years ago. This big cat is commonest in southern China and the natives in Wassu seemed unfamiliar with it.

The range of the clouded leopard (*Felis nebulosa*), is not well known. Carter believed it occurred in the Wassu country but we saw no skins and Allen (1938), recorded it only from more southern China.

Smaller mammals of intermediate size were the tiger cat (*Felis bengalensis chinensis*), and possibly the lynx (*Lynx lynx isabellind*), the pale desert cat (*Felis bieti*) not occurring in the desert as the name might imply and Teminick's cat (*Felis teminicki tristis*). We collected several fruit-eating martens (*Charronia f. flauvigua*). Red foxes and badgers (*Meles M. leptorynchus*) were common, although the latter was confined to the river valleys and open farmlands.

In the heart of the giant panda habitat we caught 1,140 small mammals. While trailing pandas through the bamboos I often observed a network of small mammal tracks.

Three hundred and fifty-six of these specimens were wild rats (*Rattus* sp.) of six species caught from the river valley bottom to the highest slopes of bamboo. We caught several bamboo rats (*Rhizomys* sp.) not included above. The bamboo rat is no more of a rat than a muskrat. It is a rodent resembling a large mole, about the size of our common muskrat, with a stub of a tail and very small eyes, and covered with dense grey soft fur.

Three hundred and fifty-one Asiatic wood mice were collected. Resembling the North American wood mouse (*Peromyscus*), these little rodents are largely nocturnal and forage on top of the snow around the base of trees and throughout the bamboos. We only caught one specimen of a long-tailed mole shrew (*Sorex scotonyx*). Two pikas were caught in rocks of the Chengo River bed and were the only ones caught below timber line.

In addition, 6 short-tailed shrews, 51 Asiatic long-tailed shrews, 78 striped-back shrews, and 227 shrew moles were captured; they also had been found at timber line and above. Twenty-six black voles (*Microtus eothenomys*), 8 striped squirrels, 12 house mice (*Mus*) and 3 moles (*Talpa Micrura*) completed the small mammals. Two Chinese minks (*Mustela sp.*) and 6 weasels (*Mustela sibirica moupenensis*) were also collected.

Presumably many of the mammals would be available to any carnivore including the giant panda.

Carter trapped 432 mammals at Tsaopo, which was at an altitude of 4,000 feet. It could be considered another zone. The only mammals caught there and not elsewhere were 35 rock squirrels (*Sciurtamias*) and one flying squirrel (*Tragopterus xanthipes*).

In Wassu the three genera of goat-antelopes (goral, serow, takin) occur as primitive members of Bovidae.

The goral is a small goatlike mammal with very short horns. It is a cliff dweller. Although found as high as 10,000 feet altitude it is most common in the more arid areas in the river gorges at 2,500–4,000 feet.

The serow, referred to throughout this book, is a large edition of the goral. Very dark, and some species having a white mane, we found them widespread in the bamboo life zone extending from timber line to the valley floors.

The most remarkable of this group is the takin, referred to by the Chinese as *yea gnu* (wild cow). Perry describes the takin as "very heavily built with short immensely thick legs and feet with a humped back, roman nose, gnu-like short horns, short ears and goat-like tail." These shy remarkable beasts with golden color are almost as much mountaineers as their cousins, the North American Rocky Mountain goat. Whereas the latter only lives above timber, the takin in Wassu ranges from about 7,000 feet to 14,500 feet in the grasslands. It is very adept at negotiating the cliffs and ledges in the bamboo jungles.

Most of the mammals in these highlands have extended their range south and west into the foothills of the main Himalaya ranges. Among the large mammals the only exception is the giant panda which remained in western Szechwan after the Pleistocene. Its range is probably more restricted than any other large mammal in western China.

Appendix II

Mammals collected by the Sage West China expedition

SPECIES	COMMON NAME
Uropsiles soricipes	Shrew Mole
Sorex excelsis	Bi-colored Shrew
Sorex argatus sihalis	Long Tailed Brown Shrew
Sorex c. cylindrica	Striped Back Shrew
Blarinella quadriticauda	Short Tailed Shrew
Sorex scotonyx	Long Tailed Mole Shrew
Anouro sorex squamipes	Mole Shrew
Sorex araneus sinalis	Brown Shrew
Sorex excelsus	Dark Grey Shrew
Soriculus spihypsobius	Long Tailed Grey Shrew
Talps micocoa longirosttis	Mole
Scaptonyx fusicaudatus	Long Tailed Mole
Rhinolophus ferrum equinum	Horshoe Bat
Rhinolophus affinis	Horshoe Bat
Rhinolophus cornutus	Horshoe Bat
Plecotus auritus	Long Eared Bat
Pipistrellus puluoratus	Pipistrel Bat
Microtus eothenomys	Black Vole
Microtus ireni	Short Tailed Brown Vole
Microtus sp.	Long Tailed Brown Vole
Apodemus sp.	Asiatic Wood Mouse
Mus	House Mouse
Rattus niviventer confusianus	Rat
Rattus andersoni	Rat
Rattus excelsior	Rat
Rattus flavipectus	Rat
Rattus Vitidus	Rat
Rattus noregicus socer	Rat
Rattus edwardsi gigas	Rat
Rhizomys sinensis sinensis	Bamboo Rat
Tamiops swinhoei swinhoei	Striped Squirrel
Sciurtamias	Rock Squirrel

SPECIES	COMMON NAME
Tragopterus xanthipes	Flying Squirrel
Ochotona Thibetana Thibetana	Pika or Mouse Hare
Felis bengalensis	Tiger Cat
Charronia F. flauviga	Marten
Lynx lynx isabellina ?	Lynx
Felis teminicki tristis ?	Teminick's Cat
Mustela sibirica moupinensis	Weasel
Mustela sp.	Chinese Mink
Meles M. leptorynchus	Badger
Ailurus fulgens stayeni	Little Red Panda
Ailuropoda Melanoleuca	Giant Panda
Selenaretos thibetanus moupinesis	Himalayan Black Bear
Vulpes v. hoolei	Red Fox
Panthera pardus	Leopard
Cuon alpinus	Wild Red Dog
Pseudois nagaar szechuanensis	Blue Sheep
Budorcas taxicolo tibetanus	Takin
Capicornis sumatrensis milne-edwardsi	Serow
Naemorhedus goral griseus	Goral
Sus scrofa moupinensi	Wild Boar
Elaphodus cephalophus cephalophus	Tufted Deer
Moschus morchiferus sifanicus	Musk Deer
Rhinopithecus roxellanae	Golden Monkey

Appendix III

Species of birds collected by the Sage West China expedition*

SPECIES	COMMON NAME
Lophophurus ihuysi	Ihuysis or Monal Pheasant (close relative of Impeyan Pheasant)
Emberiza cia ithamensis	Rock Bunting
Ithaginis sinensis annae	Mrs. Sage's Blood Pheasant
Streptopelia chinensis	Spotted Dove
Prunella strophiata strophiata	Rufous Breasted Accentor
Tarsiger chrysaeus chysaeus	Golden Bush-Robin
Tragopan temmincki	Temminck's Tragopan
Accipter gentilis	Goshawk
Ardeola bacchus	Chinese Pond Heron
Dicrurus hottentotta brevirostris	Spangled Drongo
Corvus corone orientalis	Carrion Crow
Motacilla cinera	Grey Wagtail
Buteo buteo	Buzzard
Accipter nisus nisosimilis	Sparrow Hawk
Aquila pemarina	Lesser Spotted Eagle
Pericrocutus brevirostris ethologus	Flame-coloured Minivet
Rhyacornis fuliginosus fuliginosus	Plumbeus Water Redstart
Monticola solitaria	Blue Rock Thrush
Motacilla alba hodgsoni	White Wagtail
Chaimorrornis leucocephalus	White Capped Water Redstart
Lanius schach subsp.	Black-headed Shrike
Garrulux glandarius sinensis	Jay
Falco tinnunculus interstinctus	Dark Kestrel
Garrulux cineracceus cinereiceps	Ashy Laughing Thrush
Garrulux elliotii elliotii	Elliot's Laughing Thrush
Tichodroma muraria	Wall Creeper
Falco tinnunculus stegmanni	Stegmann's Kestrel
Columbia leuconota gradaria	Snow Pigeon

* Listed in chronological order by dates collected. English names from L. Vaurie, *The Birds of the Palearctic Fauna*, 2 vols. (London: Wetherby, 1959, 1965).

SPECIES	COMMON NAME
Oenopopelia tranquebarica humilis	Ruddy Turtle Dove
Picus canus (sordidior or szetchuanensis)	Grey-headed Woodpecker
Cinclus pallasii pallasii	Brown Dipper
Enicurus scouleri	Little Forktail
Pica pica sericea	Chinese Magpie
Nucifraga caryocatactes macella	Nutcracker
Conostoma aemodius	Great Parrotbill
Saxicola ferrea laringtoni	Grey Bush Chat
Phoenicurus frontalis	Blue-fronted Redstart
Parus monticolus yunannensis	Green-Backed Tit
Pucrasia macrolopha ruficollis	Orange-collared Koklass Pheasant
Trochalopterum affinis blythii	Black-faced Laughing Thrush
Procarduelis nipalensis intensicolor	Dark Rose Finch
Babax lanceolatus lanceolatus	Chinese Babax
Glaucidium cuculoides whitelyi	Barred Owlet
Phoenicurus hodgsoni	Hodgson's Redstart
Emberiza cia subsp.	Rock Bunting
Sitta europaea montium	Chinese Nuthatch
Garrulux lunulatus	Barred Laughing Thrush
Tetraophasis obscurus	Verreaux's Monal Partridge
Phasianus colchius satscheuensis	Salihu Ring-necked Pheasant
Carpodacus thura feminina	Thura's Rose Finch
Yuhina diademata diademata	White-collared Yuhina
Moupinia poecilotis	Chestnut-tailed Moupinia
Dryocopus martius ithamensis	Black Woodpecker
Anthus spinoletta coutellii	Water Pipit
Troglodytes t. szetschuanus	Wren
Tarsiger indicus yunnanensis	White-Growed Bush Robin
Alcippe cinereiceps cinereiceps	Grey-headed Tit Babbler
Carpodacus edwardsii edwardsii	Rosey Finch
Grandala coelicolor	Grandala
Chrysolophus pictus	Golden Pheasant
Carpodacus trifasciata	Three-banded Rosey Finch
Anthus Hodgsoni hodgsoni	Indian Tree Pipit
Picoides tridactyla (funebris)	Three-toed Woodpecker
Dendrocopos darjellensis desmursi	Darjeeling Pied Woodpecker
Parus dichrous wellsi	Brown-crested Tit
Dendrocopos cathpharius	Lesser Red Woodpecker

SPECIES	COMMON NAME
Parus davidi	Père David's Tit
Aegithaliscus iouschistos bonva-	
loti	Blyth's Long-tailed Tit
Gallinaga solitaria	Solitary Snipe
Cinclus cinclus przewalskii	Dipper
Pteruthius xanthochloris pallidus	Green Shrike Babbler
Alcippe chrysotis swinhoi	Golden-Breasted Tit Babbler
Enicurus scouleri	Little Forktail
Purrhula erythaca	Bearan's Bull Finch
Turdus naumanni naumanni	Naumann's Thrush
Turdus merula subsp.	Chinese Black Thrush
Dendrocopos major cabanisi	Great-spotted Woodpecker
Parus major altarum	Great Tit
Alcedo atthis bengalensis	Kingfisher
Picus canus	Green Woodpecker
Motacilla cinerea	Grey Wagtail
Tarsiger cyanurus rufilatus	Red-flanked Bluetail
Pheoni curus auroreus auroreus	Daurian Redstart
Lanius schach schach	Black-headed Shrike
Passer montanus iubilaeus	Tree Sparrow
Passer rutilans rutilans	Cinnamon Sparrow

Selected Bibliography

ALLEN, GLOVER M. 1938. *The Mammals of China and Mongolia,* vol. 11, Part 1. New York: *Am. Mus. of Nat. Hist.*

BROCKLEHURST, H. C. 1938. *The Giant Panda.* London: Field CLXXI.

CARTER, T. D. 1937. The Giant Panda. *Bull. New York Zool. Soc.* 40: 6–14.

COLBERT, E. H. 1938. The Panda: A Study in Emigration. *Nat. Hist.* 42: 33–39.

COLLINS, LARRY R., and JAMES K. PAGE, JR. 1973. *Ling-Ling and Hsing-Hsing: Year of the Panda.* Garden City, New York: Doubleday, Anchor Press.

DAVID, A. 1889. *Le Faune Chinoise.* Paris: Bureaux des Ann. Phil. Chret.

DAVIS, D. D. 1964. The Giant Panda: A Morphological Study of Evolutionary Mechanisms. *Fieldiana: Zool. Mem.* 3: 1–339.

EDGAR, J. 1932. The First Prince of Washii or Wassu. *Journ. of the West China Border Research Society,* pp 73–74.

GRAHAM, D. C. 1942. How The Baby Pandas Were Captured. *Bull. New York Zool. Soc.* 45: 19–23.

GREGORY, W. K. 1936. *On the Phylogenetic Relationships of the Giant Panda* (Auluropeda) *To Other Arctoid Carnivora.* Am. Mus. of Nat. Hist., N.Y., Novitates, no. 878, pp 19–23.

HARKNESS, R. 1938. *The Lady and the Panda.* London: Nicholoson and Watson.

KAN, O., and T. SHU-HUA. 1964. In The Peking Zoo—The First Baby Giant Panda. *Bull. New York Zool. Soc.* 67: 44–46.

LYDEKKER, R. 1901. Detailed Description of the Skull and Limbbones (of *Ailuropoda melanoleuca*). *Trans. Linn. Society London* (2) 8: 166–71.

MATTHEW, W. D., and W. GRANGER. 1923. New Fossil Mammals from the Pliocene of Szechuan. *China Bull., Amer. Mus. of Nat. Hist., N.Y.* 48 (17): 563–98.

MILNE, EDWARDS. 1868–74. *Recherches Pour Setuit a L'Histoire Naturelle Des Mamifères,* vol. 1. Paris: Masson, pp. 321–28.

―――. 1869. Extrait d'une Lettre de Même (M. l'Abbe David) datée de la Principalité Thibétaine (independante) de Moupin, le 21 Mars 1869. *Nouv. Arch. Mus. Nat. Hist. Paris* 5 (bulletin): 13.

MORRIS, DESMOND, and RAMONA MORRIS. 1966. *Men and Panda.* New York: McGraw-Hill.

NELSON, E. W. 1918. Wild Animals of North America. *Nat. Geog.,* Nov. 1916 (pt. 1), May 1918 (pt. 2).

PEN, H-S. 1943. Some Notes on the Giant Panda. *Bull. Fan. Mem. Inst. Biol. Peiping*, n.s. 1 (1): 64–70.

———. 1962. Animals of Western Szechuan. *Nature*, Oct. 6, 1962.

PERRY, RICHARD. 1969. *The World of the Giant Panda*. N.Y.: Taplinger Pub. Co.

POCOCK, R. I. 1921. The External Characters and Classification of Procyonidae. *Proc. 2001 Soc. London*, pp. 389–422.

———. 1946. The Panda and The Giant Panda. *Zoo Life* 1: 67–70.

RAVEN, H. C. 1936. Notes on the Anatomy and Viscera of the Giant Panda *(Ailuropoda Melanoleuca). Am. Mus. Novitates*, no. 877, pp. 1–23.

ROOSEVELT, T., and K. ROOSEVELT. 1929. *Trailing the Giant Panda*. N.Y.: Scribner's.

SAGE, DEAN, JR. 1935. In Quest of the Giant Panda. *Nat. Hist., Am. Mus. of Nat. Hist., N.Y.* 35: 309–20.

SARICH, VINCENT. 1973. Giant Pandas in a Biochemical Laboratory. *Nat. Hist., Am. Mus. of Nat. Hist., N.Y.* 82, no. 10: 72–73.

SCHAFER, E. 1938. Der Bambusbar *(Ailuropoda melanoleuca). Zool. Garten*, Leipzig 10, pp. 21–31.

———. 1972–73. Various personal letters to author cited in text.

SCHALLER, GEORGE B. 1973. On the Behavior of Blue Sheep *(Pseudois Nayaur). Journ. of the Bombay Nat. Hist. Society* 69, no. 3, pp. 523–37.

SHELDON, W. G. 1937. Notes on the Giant Panda. *Journ. of Mammal* 18: 13–19.

SMITH, FLOYD TANGIER. 1937. Copies of personal letters to his sister about giant pandas. U.S. Library of Congress.

SWAN, LAWRENCE W. 1961. The Ecology of the High Himalayas. *Sci. Amer.* 205 (4): 68–78.

SUNG WANG, and LU CHANG-KUN. 1973. Giant Pandas in the Wild. *Nat. Hist., Am. Mus. of Nat. Hist., N.Y.* 82, no. 10, pp. 70–71.

TORRANCE, T. 1932. Notes on the West China Aboriginal Tribes. *Journ. of the West China Border Research Society*, pp. 10–24.

WEIGOLD, H. 1924. Weitere Bemerkungen, Dr. Weigolds Zu den Gesammelten Säugetieren in Zool. Ergeb. Walter. Stötzners' Exped. *Szetschwan Abn. Ber. Mus. Dresden* 16 (2): 71–76.

WILSON, E. H. 1908. The Chinese Flora. *Journ. Roy. Hort. Soc., London*, pp. 395–400.

———. 1913. *A Naturalist in Western China*. 2 vols. London: Methuen.

Index